Hiring Revolution is dedicated to all of the people who did and didn't hire us throughout the past twenty-five years of our working lives.

Those lived experiences—both good and bad—shaped how we approach building big, brave, mixed, impactful dream teams!

HIRING

REVOLUTION

A GUIDE TO DISRUPT
RACISM AND SEXISM
IN HIRING

TRINA C. OLSON & ALFONSO T. WENKER

ISBN 13: 978-1-63489-465-4

Library of Congress Catalog Number has been applied for.
Printed in the United States of America
First Printing: 2021
25 24 23 22 21   5 4 3 2 1

Cover design by Zoe Norvell
Interior design by Cindy Samargia Laun
Citation formatting by Maria Isabel Gonzalez

Wise Ink Creative Publishing
807 Broadway St. NE, Suite 46
Minneapolis, MN 55413
wiseink.com

CONTENTS

PREFACE

Well, here we are. Or, there we were. The first draft of the manuscript for *Hiring Revolution* was due one week after our home state of Minnesota issued its stay-home order in response to the pandemic. We first put proverbial pen to paper about nine months before public businesses and schools across the land now called the United States started to close down to slow the spread of COVID-19. This gave us pause. Would this particular Hiring Revolution be needed in the same way? We reflected on it, grappled with it, and received incredible counsel from our publishing partner Dara at Wise Ink. Yes, we concluded, and if nothing else, the revolution would be more possible and likely more welcome when organizations that hire workers returned to "normal" function and needed to hire in new and different ways.

In the midst of our first round of edits, on May 25, 2020, George Floyd, a Black man, was publicly murdered by Minneapolis police officers. Our city became the epicenter of an uprising against state-sanctioned violence against Black bodies. The uprising wasn't a new or even renewed response; it was another natural overflow of generations of pain, rising to meet the gravity of the violent white supremacist reality we live in. Young Black leaders, queer and trans Black leaders, and working poor Black leaders, whose outrage and calls for dignity have gone unheard since the earliest notions of this "country," led the public outcry. Activists, organizers, and those new to movements for progress took to the streets, donated money and supplies, set up organic structures, and doubled down on Black-led organizing. Thanks to long-term work led by Black organizers and accelerated by the murder of Mr. Floyd, a supermajority of our city council stood in a park on a Sunday afternoon and promised to defund and deconstruct the police and reimagine with the community what public safety could be like. That struggle continues.

While we write this very preface, the West Coast lands now called California, Oregon, and Washington are recovering from record-breaking wildfires caused by human irresponsibility, in both the initial sparks of individual fires and the climate change–driven drought that encouraged their spread. The skies were orange, residents could not breathe, and thousands were displaced and lost the homes and communities where they make family.

The week before this writing, Supreme Court Associate Justice Ruth Bader Ginsburg passed away less than fifty days before Election Day, leaving us wondering about the future of reproductive, civil, and human rights protections.

We offer *Hiring Revolution* in the midst of concurrent crises—not surprises, but rather predictable outcomes of generations of neglect: a federal administration's bombastic, willful disregard for foresight and management of a pandemic; the legacy of slavery and the racist history of policing; the fossil fuel industry's dominance of our economy. A pandemic, a racialized uprising, and climate change are predictable results of structures designed to extract labor and resources for the benefit of a small handful of wealth hoarders.

We offer *Hiring Revolution* in pursuit of a shift:

- Away from economies of extraction and toward a new way of hiring and valuing workers across multiple races and genders.
- Away from racist and sexist hiring practices that prefer the white masculine and toward a collective experience of being hired to contribute creatively from a place of race and gender as assets.
- Away from the control and subjugation of Black, brown, feminine, and nonconforming worker bodies and toward a celebration and valuing of the contribution of all bodies.

We offer *Hiring Revolution* because we know this revolution is possible. Because it's time to stop asking, "How can I diversify my candidate pool?" and stop saying, "There aren't any qualified People of Color, women, or trans folks for this role," and acknowledge that racism and sexism were set up on purpose for us to believe those lies.

In a June 2020 memo and a September 2020 Zoom call, the CEO of Wells Fargo stated that he believed the reason their company, and the financial sector as a whole, was not racially diverse was that there is limited Black talent to fill those rolls. When his writing and statement became public, a conversation was reignited about hiring pipelines, personal capacity, and the ways that unconscious biases drive thought patterns, strategies, and decisions. "Perhaps it is the CEO of Wells Fargo who lacks the talent to recruit Black workers," said Rep. Alexandria Ocasio-Cortez on Twitter.[1] Well said, Congresswoman!

---

1   Ken Sweet, "Wells Fargo CEO Apologizes for Comments about Diversity," AP News, September 23, 2020, https://apnews.com/article/archive-charles-scharf-fa3ea27361567b3cf1f4c011467194ec.

Hiring Revolution wasn't the book we thought we would write first, but those questions and statements kept coming. So now we're ready to share the revolution with you. **This book is an offer to be used in its wholeness.** The revolution is not a buffet, nor can you get it à la carte. To truly and completely upend racist and sexist hiring practices, you'll need to read the whole thing, answer all the reflection questions, use all the tools, and practice what you have learned after you close the book.

Read this if you believe you can change. Don't read this if you want to stew in admiration of your problems.

Read this if you believe your colleagues and your company can change. Don't read this if you'd prefer to point fingers at your workplace and think that only others have to change.

Read this if you believe in possibility. Don't read this if you're not ready to try things out.

Read this if you want to be part of the shifts away from racism and sexism. Don't read this if you don't believe structural racism and sexism exist.

Welcome to the *Hiring Revolution*.

INTRODUCTION

A MORAL IMPERATIVE + GOOD BUSINESS SENSE

This is not the book we thought we'd write first. But you kept asking, *How do we diversify our candidate pool for hiring?* We know how to help.

In recent years, people inside the American workforce seem to have woken up, looked around, and realized that most of the faces looking back at them were similar to their own. We're glad folks have finally noticed this very unstrategic "norm."

Homogeneity is NOT the birth of innovation.

Whole companies, regardless of their espoused racial and gender diversity goals, are genuinely struggling with how to consistently and effectively recruit, hire, and retain top talent that includes Black, Indigenous, People of Color, women, and gender nonbinary/gender-nonconforming leaders. Especially when it comes to hiring into positions of authority (think vice presidents, directors, managers, and those in the C-suite), members of these groups get passed over—their talents, perspectives, and experiences dismissed—in favor of hiring and promoting white men into these pivotal positions. White men are not magically the only humans capable of running teams, projects, and whole companies. It's preposterous.

Are current hiring practices ethical or desirable? NO!

You've chosen to pick up this book, so we know that you are troubled by the staggering race and gender disparities in hiring. Before we lay out our approach to the Hiring Revolution, it's important to situate ourselves inside the truth. Context is important, and if we're going to fix something we must be precise about the problem. Two facts make up the foundation of the revolution:

- **Bias**—the preference for whiteness and masculinity—is a serious problem currently baked into traditional hiring processes.
- Current hiring norms **limit** and **harm** both individuals and businesses.

In order to produce different workforce outcomes, we must carefully consider the preferences for whiteness and masculinity and the barriers facing certain kinds of workers (namely People of Color, women, and trans people) in old-school hiring processes. Then we must reimagine and cocreate new hiring processes that align with our vision, values, mission, and goals. It is natural, normal, and necessary that we evolve!

"Do the best you can until you know better.
Then, when you know better, do better."
—DR. MAYA ANGELOU, POET, DANCER, PRODUCER, PLAYWRIGHT, DIRECTOR, AUTHOR

STOP, START, DO MORE, DO LESS, DO DIFFERENTLY

This sounds imposing, but the good news is that you—yes, you!—have the power to make an enormous difference!

In this book, we break down what we, Alfonso and Trina, have done to find and hire teams of people that are incredibly diverse—across race, gender identity, sexual orientation, religious tradition, age, ability, ethnicity, immigration experience, and more. *Hiring Revolution* is an invitation to stop, start, do more of, do less of, and do differently. It is a **purposefully tactical approach** to hiring the team you claim you want.

Through a thoughtful reimagining of team building, you will begin the process of reckoning with all the times and places where **your hiring intent (finding "the best," "most qualified" workers) did not ultimately match your impact** (inadvertently convincing yourself that white male workers were the best choice). We will explore small, medium, and large shifts that can transform your hiring practices toward a more equitable way of doing business. We are *not* going to spend these pages pointing out everything we've all done wrong in hiring days past. We will, instead, identify specific problems and pair each with a viable solution you could start implementing today.

Our lens of inquiry is, what could you stop, start, do more, do less, do differently?

WELCOME TO OUR EMBODIED IDENTITY HOUSE
You're Invited over Any Time—We're Glad to Have You Drop By!

Before we get started, you'll need a tour of our house. The Embodied Identity House is a model we developed and use throughout our practice. It helps us build a shared understanding of how core parts of our identity shape how we experience our lives.

Our company, Team Dynamics, commissioned this graphic from illustrator Cori Nakamura Lin after we got inspired at a 2016 conference in Atlanta. Building upon the decades-long conversation about intersectionality, a term coined in 1989 by professor Kimberlé Crenshaw, we wanted to paint a clear picture of the myriad ways in which our human differences make a difference in our lived experiences.

Each of us lives in a "house" such as the one shown here. However each of us envisions this identity house—apartment, house, dorm, temporary shelter of all sorts, and so on—all of these rooms are always present. Loosely, the nine rooms in our graphic represent core protected classes in the US. What does that mean? It means that bias, discrimination, prejudice, harassment, and even violence have been perpetrated against people simply because of these facets of their identity. The order in which the rooms appear is not important and might change in your own vision of the house; the attic is not more or less important than the basement.

All of these rooms are always present in our house, even when we might feel that we're occupying only one. You can close a door and pull the blinds, but the room is still there, still affecting the overall comfort and function of the whole house. For example:

> *Alfonso:* I am not "just" a millennial. I am a third-generation Mexican American, gay, millennial man.
> *Trina:* I am not "just" a woman. I am a white, queer woman who has changed economic class in my lifetime and has a hidden disability.

We are not "just" business partners and friends. We are in a meaningful and important financial and vocational relationship across race, gender, ethnicity, and more.

You get our points?
1. Each of us is *always* our whole house.
2. In different settings, we feel more or less aware of certain parts of our identity.
3. Facets of our identity experience praise, pride, and pain.

Which parts of our identity are feeling activated or dormant at any one moment depends entirely on our context: who we are around and the ways we are feeling safe and unsafe, valued and ignored.

You will undoubtedly notice that the race door is shaded in the graphic. In the United States, **race is currently the factor making the most significant difference** in how people are talked about and treated; and race, in combination with any of the other rooms in the house, leads to even worse outcomes for those who are Black, Indigenous, or People of Color compared to white people who share those identities. For example:

- A white, light-skinned, and/or white-passing immigrant to the United States has a better experience than an immigrant of color.
- A Black transgender woman is at a higher risk of violence than a white transgender woman.
- A white person with a physical disability gets better care than a disabled Person of Color.

We invite you into the Embodied Identity House to give you a grounding in why the Hiring Revolution must be centered in race. Not because race is politically "hot" right now or because it's "politically correct" to be supportive of diversity, equity, and inclusion efforts, but instead **because it is both logical and imperative to begin where the most egregious wrongs are being perpetrated. Right now, that's race.**

ACTIVITY—DRAW YOUR "HOUSE"

This will take less than five minutes and inform the rest of your reading of Hiring Revolution. *Please take the time!*

1) Grab a pen or pencil. If you are cool with writing in this book (we're cool with it, by the way), answer here; if you'd prefer a blank page, find one. Now draw a dwelling that reminds you of home. It can be an apartment building, a trailer, your grandma's house—whatever works for you.

Draw nine rooms and one door. This doesn't have to be an architectural masterpiece, but if a ruler makes you feel better, go for it. Label the door "Race" and label the nine rooms, in whatever order you like, with the following: immigration, language, class, religion/faith, age, ability, gender, sexuality, ethnicity.

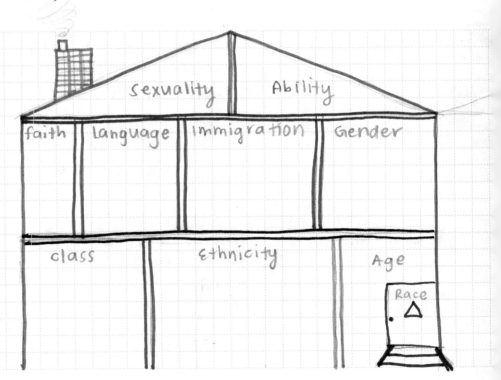

2) In each room and the door, **write down the words you currently use to describe your own sense of each of these identities.** Don't fixate on the words you've seen on forms, including the Census. Day to day, how do you actually describe yourself? You can use more than one word, and you are welcome to write in whatever language(s) flows best for you.

Alfonso: I would currently write, from the top to the bottom of the house: I am a US-born US citizen; I can only speak English fluently; my current household income is over $100K; I have an anxiety disorder and am currently able-bodied; I was born in 1986; I was raised Catholic and still consider myself Christian; I use the words *gay* and *queer* to describe my sexuality; I am a cisgender man—assigned male at birth, growing up as a boy, and now identifying as a man; my mom is Mexican, my dad is German; depending on who I'm talking to, I use the words *Latino*, *Latinx*, and *third-generation Mexican American* to describe my racial identity.

sexuality: bicurious

ability: able-bodied, anxious

faith: catholic raised but agnostic / spiritual

language: English only

immigration: US born and raised / not an immigrant

gender: cis woman

class: upper middle class family but working class on my own

ethnicity: German, welsh, English

age: mid-20s, millennial cusper

race: white (European descent)

3) As you review the words you just wrote down, **reflect on how you currently feel about those words.** Do you feel close to them? Far away? Proud? Embarrassed? Unsure? Are some of your identity words currently in flux, and are you trying out new ones? Practice noticing your own feelings about your relationship to the various facets of your lived identities.

4) *Think about how you've felt at work when participating in hiring efforts in the past (either trying to get hired or doing the hiring). Now circle the three parts of your Embodied Identity House that **were most in your awareness** during that process. Why do you think that was? Which three were you least cognizant of?*

most

least

race, age and ability / faith, sexuality +
ethnic.

5) *Lastly, what **impacts and unintended consequences** might you experience when the three identities most present to you are the ones others in your work example thought least about, and vice versa?*

5.a. may not think about my privileges or blind spot
as a white, young able bodied person

5b. Discrimination based on sexuality or religion

For more detail and activities related to the Embodied Identity House, go to www.TeamDynamicsMN.com/tools

*In 2016, we attended a meeting of philanthropic
leaders in Atlanta to discuss increasing funding to
LGBTQ+ (Lesbian, Gay, Bisexual, Transgender, Queer)
leaders and organizations. Given our southern context, we
explored the intersection of racial justice and LGBTQ+ justice.
Our colleague Marcus Walton (now CEO of Grantmakers
for Effective Organizations) provided a helpful mental image
that spurred the creation of our Embodied Identity House
when he said:*

*"When having conversations about
equity, I don't need us to live only in a race house,
but I do need us to come through a race door."*
–MARCUS WALTON, CEO OF GRANTMAKERS FOR EFFECTIVE ORGANIZATIONS

KEY TERMS

A BRIEF DISCUSSION OF TERMINOLOGY AND VOCABULARY

In this book, we're focused on the hiring experience of People of Color, women, and trans people. That's the phrase we're going to use frequently. People are pretty freaked out about using the "right" words when it comes to talking about racism and sexism. No one wants to "get it wrong." But it also feels like words and phrases are changing so rapidly! How is a person supposed to keep up?

Here's the truth: words are important; words are meaningful; and words and phrases related to culture and identity are in constant flux. Their meanings live in impermanence. Our approach here is *not* to define words in the English language once and for all. Rather, we want to **create shared meaning** between you and us. How we use language changes often, even from day to day, and members of different groups, or even members of the same group, may not agree on word choice. These are the words we use; if members of your team or potential hires express a preference for other terms, listen to and respect their preferences.

As you read, keep in mind two key concepts of language use:

1. While we use terms to discuss groups of people, we know that these are not monolithic groups with identical experiences.
2. Discrimination at the intersection of race and gender (such as for trans Women of Color) compounds the devastating effects of underhiring, resulting in current and historical poverty.

WORDS + PHRASES WE USE IN THIS BOOK

Hiring Revolution uses a set of words and phrases to describe groups of people, conditions those groups experience, and the nature in which cultural behavior influences hiring practices and outcomes. What follows is the linguistic sandbox we developed for this distinct project. This list is not in alphabetical order. Instead, it is grouped by related concepts. The language and definitions we share here are both imperfect and specific: these are the words and phrases we need access to in order to spark the Hiring Revolution.

We compiled this list with gratitude to activists, scholars, thought leaders, and revolutionaries who, throughout time, have sought to put language to the lived experience of socially constructed realities such as race, class, and gender. So, with enthusiasm and humility, we offer this English-language container to guide our work together toward our individual and collective revolution!

Race and gender are made up AND real in their consequences. Sit with that a minute. It's wild. Say it out loud if it helps you slow down and allow this strange duality to sink in.

Social identity markers such as race and gender have been used by societies in recent centuries to define belonging to a group that shares a sense of connectivity. Historically, it was most common to identify first with one's own geography (for example, Rome) or religious practices (such as Islam) as a way of making sense of who someone was and to whom they were connected. The rise of European imperialism brought with it a need to create social stratification **defined by lightness and darkness of skin**, as well as the societal expectations of a **binary differentiation between men/boys and women/girls.**[2]

When we talk about race in the twenty-first century, we're typically referring to a whole host of characteristics (skin color, hair texture, facial features, and more). In a historic and modern American context, race refers to the intentional construction of social hierarchy based on the darkness of one's skin. The lighter, the better. The preference for lightness over darkness is colorism. (If you need to, set this book down for thirty seconds and shake this grossness out of your body. You're also welcome to give your disgust and disappointment sound. Make some noise—it won't hurt anybody to say a bunch of swear words in a row to get it out. Try "Damnit, damnit, damnit, damnit, damnit!" This is part of our practice when we've had to listen to lies that have taken hold and hurt ourselves and our friends. Try it!)

When discussing race in the United States, we often think about racialized categories with names including (but not limited to) Black, Indigenous, Latinx,

---

2   For more background on this shift, see Nell Irvin Painter, *The History of White People* (New York: W. W. Norton & Company, 2011).

Asian Pacific Islander, North African/Arab/Middle Eastern, and white. A mix of characteristics, including skin pigment, hair color, hair texture, eye shape, and shape of nose and lips, have been used to try to jam individuals with whole histories and complex family lineages into tidy racialized categories, thus inferring a ton about the conflation of race with a person's inherent value and right to dignity.

This construction of race and its rank ordering of associated characteristics rely on racism to enforce a hierarchy of human value wherein whiteness is preferred over all other races. Racism, as defined by leaders and scholars Gita Gulati-Partee and Maggie Potapchuk, refers to **_history, policy, culture, practice, and belief to maintain a racial hierarchy._** In the US context, this racial hierarchy is organized with white people at the top. Hiring practices prefer white people and the associated behaviors of whiteness that often get coded as "professional," "appropriate," and "ideal." The Hiring Revolution requires that we upend our workplace preferences for white people and behaviors associated with whiteness as universally supreme.

Today, it is crystal clear that zero reputable science supports the claim that any one race is genetically (physically, intellectually, emotionally) superior to any other.[3] **It's important to recognize, as we rumble with race and racism in today's workplaces, that centuries of junk science have been used to "prove" the inferiority of People of Color and the superiority of white people.** From Nazis preaching dehumanizing propaganda about the superiority of a light-skinned, light-eyed, light-haired, Christian "Master Race" to early pseudo-anthropologists fabricating a hierarchy of three racial categories based on human skull measurements, white supremacists have consistently and effectively peddled racist propaganda.

Although the science on race is clear, giving up a racialized hierarchy remains hard for some people because we have been personally, institutionally, and structurally programmed to believe otherwise. We have all ingested millions of pieces of data defining whose bodies are dangerous, whose customs are

---

3   For more background, see: Ibram X. Kendi, _Stamped from the Beginning: The Definitive History of Racist Ideas in America_ (New York: Bold Type Books, 2017); Nell Irvin Painter, _The History of White People_ (New York: W. W. Norton, 2011); and Dorothy Roberts, _Fatal Invention: How Science, Politics, and Big Business Re-create Race in the 21st Century_ (New York: New Press, 2012).

"backward," and who is more and less intellectually capable. We have a lot of unlearning to do, at the deepest psychological levels, in order to reroute our neurological pathways, catch our preferences for whiteness in action, and behave more in accordance with our values and what we know to be true.

Gender refers to the three-part combination of our sense of self (identity), the way we outwardly express that sense of self (expression), and how we choose to or are expected to participate in a group or community (role), all in the context of how masculinity and femininity are defined, valued, and enforced.

Gender Identity can be explained as our knowledge of who we are in terms of gender and the words we choose to describe our own gender. Most often we think of only two genders: woman and man. However, there is a vast multitude of ways to refer to one's own gender. People whose gender identity does not fit neatly inside US society's two gender boxes use many different terms, but collectively they are often referred to as nonbinary people. For example, Jonathan Van Ness, from the hit TV show *Queer Eye*, is nonbinary.

Our insistence on only two gender identities at best limits creative personal expression and at worst creates the conditions in which gender violence and discrimination limit the health and success of women and nonbinary people. Additionally, the limited view of only two genders is a particularly white framework. For millennia, different cultures recognized, and even celebrated, a gender spectrum and variance in gender identities, including recognition of various Indigenous communities of two-spirit people and recognition in India of a third gender known as hijra.

In the United States today, words and phrases for identity broadly fall into two umbrella categories: transgender and cisgender.

Transgender folks are people whose gender identity does *not* match the biological sex (female/male) they were assigned at birth. **Cisgender** refers to folks whose gender identity matches the biological sex they were assigned at birth.

> *Alfonso:* For example, when I was born, it was proclaimed, "It's a boy!" I was raised as a boy and conditioned as a man, and I call myself and live as a man.

The insistence that there are only two genders limits our hiring opportunities because it demands we categorize people into two limiting boxes with the assumption that everyone in each box is having the same lived experience. Additionally, the US workplace has developed a set of leadership qualities and images that presume men to be more capable, professional, and likely to possess leadership qualities, thus resulting in increased hiring, paying, and promoting of men in the workplace. Further, the preference is for masculine-presenting men above all other qualities and behaviors.

The revolution requires the destruction of the binary and an expansive reimagining of the various and varied capable bodies leadership comes in. Throughout the book we'll talk about the disparate impact of existing hiring practices on women and nonbinary people. When we talk about women we mean both transgender and cisgender women. We are also aware that nonbinary people consistently experience lower rates of hiring because of their nonbinary identity and expression.

Gender Expression is primarily about our outward expressions of femininity and masculinity. Dominant assumptions about gender expression assume each one of us is singularly "more feminine" or "more masculine" all the time and that, given our gender identity, we use a narrow set of ways to express ourselves. For example, at work, women and nonbinary folks "can wear skirts, dresses, or pants," and men "should wear pants." Why? What does the fabric covering our lower bodies matter? How does it limit or make it more or less possible for a worker to do their job? In the workplace, traits we tend to describe as "ideal leadership qualities" and "professionalism" are associated with masculine-categorized behaviors, while we diminish leadership behaviors currently associated with the idea of femininity.

The American workplace prefers masculinity so strongly that masculine-presenting people and men get hired, paid, and promoted more,[4] and those who prefer a more feminine expression are expected to perform masculinity to get ahead in the workplace; which sucks.

---

4   "Men 40 Percent More Likely Than Women to Be Promoted in Management Roles," *Engage Employee*, August 25, 2020, https://engageemployee.com/men-40-percent-likely-women-promoted-management-roles/.

The Hiring Revolution demands we end this preference for masculinity, develop a broad set of desired leadership qualities, and authentically value them across a spectrum of femininity and masculinity.

Gender Roles are about a group's or society's expectations of what is okay and not okay for people of a certain gender to do or perform. For example, we expect men to be good at "money stuff" in the workplace and women and nonbinary folks to be good at "managing interpersonal disputes" (eyeroll!).

Gender roles in the workplace are limiting to our workers, teams, and businesses because they 1) are based in a false binary that there are only men and women and those identities are supposed to be good and bad at only certain work tasks, and 2) limit the menu of options for skills we might expect workers of various genders to build. The Hiring Revolution expects that assumptions about gender roles will be replaced by a shared set of expectations about what we need our next hires to be able to do, create, and learn.

Preference for Whiteness and Masculinity: Patterns of choice and decision-making assign higher value to white people and white-coded behaviors and to men and masculine-coded behaviors, even though work can be performed by people of any and every race and gender. As a result, masculinity is preferred over feminine-coded behaviors, and white people and white-coded behaviors are preferred over Black and brown bodies and behaviors.

Racist and Sexist Hiring Practices: Patterns of hiring reinforce a hierarchy of human value sustaining the false idea that white people and men are better, more equipped, more capable, and more professional. This results in predictable wealth disparities, both now and in the past, between People of Color and white people and between men and women/nonbinary/trans people.

We consciously and on purpose use the word "sexist" in this book because our assessment of the US workplace indicates that the current practices are situated inside an assumed biological binary without great awareness of or appreciation for the expansive possibilities of gender. We also understand sexism as a root of homophobia and transphobia (with gratitude to the generation-defining work of Suzanne Pharr), among other problems.

These racist and sexist norms create societies, and thus workplaces, where the white and masculine is supreme, whether we personally believe it is or not. Dominance continues to dominate (infuriating!).

Gender Discrimination and Violence: Women and trans people are targeted by people and structures in predictable ways for the infliction of physical, mental, or emotional pain because of their gender identity and expression. They are also underhired, underpaid, and underpromoted system wide; this is discrimination.

Race in Print: We capitalize the terms *Black*, *Indigenous*, and *People of Color*, and other terms for ethnic identity, to acknowledge that active power dynamic in printed English, while keeping *white* lowercase as a way to help other white allies and accomplices in divesting themselves of the weight of an uppercase *W*. Too often in the United States and its colonies has *white* been followed by the words *power, culture, heritage,* and ultimately *supremacy* as a means to establish power.

People of Color: When we say *People of Color*, we refer to our current understanding of who is and isn't considered and treated as white in the United States. We capitalize the *P* and the *C*. Right now, in our awareness, *People of Color* as an umbrella term includes people with Black and brown bodies who might also identify as Black, African American, African, North African/Arab/Middle Eastern, Indigenous/Native American, Alaskan, Hawaiian, Latino/a or Latinx, or Asian Pacific Islander.

White People: When we refer to white people, we mean folks in the US who have the experience of being perceived as, live as, and benefit from being considered white. We lowercase *white* when referring to it as a race. When referring to White Nationalists we will capitalize white. Otherwise, white is lowercase in this text as white has not been claimed as a culture, racial identity, or experience in the same way that being Black has. This is separate and distinct from the complexity and richness of ethnicity and familial and/or religious tradition.

Trina: For example, I am a white person. I am ethnically Scandinavian. I was raised Lutheran. When I need something from a hospital, bank, school, or member of law enforcement, I receive all the rights, privileges, and assumptions of me being a white person. In those moments it does not make a difference whether folks think I am German, English, Australian, or Norwegian: I'm treated as a white person. Nothing about acknowledging my white identity, and my associated white privilege, takes away from my being Norwegian, Swedish, and Christian as well as white. The truth is, I am treated as my race far more than I am my ethnicity. It's a both/and.

We know that who has and has not been able to claim whiteness or white identity in the United States has been and continues to be in flux. We recognize that many people's families and ancestors have been considered white, and then not, off and on throughout history. That can feel incredibly confusing, frustrating, and unsettling. Who gets invited onto and kicked off the "white people team" is ever changing! **Different geographic origins, ethnicities, and traditions have been targets for discrimination and violence throughout US colonial history.** We recognize that many white people fled their nations of origin, or were forced to leave, because they were being harassed, starved, or even murdered. While painful, these horrors are distinct from the devastating projects of US race and racism. For example, we know that Jewish, Irish, Armenian, and Italian people, among many others, have been intermittently considered both white and not white in the US. At present, many who fall into those categories, though not all, currently receive the benefits of whiteness the vast majority of the time.

Remember that categories may be helpful tools, but they do not fully represent the complexity of real human lives. Individual people often fall into more than one category: Jewish people may also be Black, white, Indigenous, or People of Color. Armenian people may have lighter or darker skin that changes their relationship to categories involving whiteness. Categories are not monolithic: people who fall into them are not an undifferentiated mass that can be only one way. We must acknowledge the beautiful diversity of human experience even as we deploy categories to understand our relationships with each other.

Who is perceived or assumed to be white or a Person of Color shifts within geographic context and in relationship to the lightness or darkness of one's own skin. We're holding that complexity with you and inviting you into the understanding that preferences for white people and whiteness are at play in every United States workplace.

> *Alfonso:* I am a light-skinned Mexican American with a brown, ethnically Mexican mom and a white, ethnically German dad. Depending on time of year and how much time I've spent in the sun, my skin color ranges from beige to olive to a toasty brown color. Depending on where I am in the United States and who I am with, folks make different assumptions about if I am white or not. However, I identify as a third-generation Mexican American, Latinx Person of Color.

White Supremacy: This long-term project aims to establish and keep white people (and white behaviors) at the top of a made-up human hierarchy for the explicit and intentional purpose of controlling land, labor, and the economy. White supremacy is a framework designed and executed to benefit white people over all others through the murder, dislocation, subjugation, and exploitation of People of Color. In the Americas, it began with the forced migration and attempted genocide of the Indigenous people who had inhabited these lands for millennia. It continued with the stealing of African and Caribbean people for the dehumanizing purposes of serving as chattel slaves. Throughout US history, it continued in extracting labor, at the lowest possible wages and in terrible conditions, from immigrants, asylum seekers, and refugees, especially those from what is now considered Mexico, Central America, South America, Africa, Asia, and the Pacific Islands.

To this day, being white confers the identity status through which one is afforded the largest and most consistent financial and health benefits (both personally and in the form of wealth and opportunity accumulation from one generation to the next).

The Southern Poverty Law Center, known by many as an expert source tracking US hate groups and domestic terrorists, defines **White Nationalism** as a movement based in white supremacy and white separatism. The White Nationalism movement is about establishing a "pure and powerful white ruling race" (yuck!). White Nationalism relies on its close cousin white supremacy for a unique distinction wherein Jewish people (many of whom experience being perceived as white and benefiting from white skin in the US) are used as scapegoats in an openly anti-Semitic way for what White Nationalists consider major societal ills—in particular, the ebb and flow of the economy.

Throughout *Hiring Revolution* we will talk about your candidate pool "mix." In HR this is often referred to as "diversity," but when we talk about mix we mean the fact of human difference. Whenever two people are together, a "diversity" of identities is present. But not every aspect of our mix of identities has the same impact. For example, **our difference in race has a greater effect on our experience of job seeking, job having, and equitable pay** than our difference in height or hair color. We acknowledge, neutrally and regardless of how we wish the world were, that *certain differences make a difference*.

KEY TAKEAWAYS

Language is always on the move. If you feel a bit lost in a maze of new terminology, take a moment to breathe. We hope you will refer back to this list as needed as you read, and with practice the terms will help you communicate clearly and with precision. You don't have to memorize the list! Our goal is for everyone reading this book to stop dancing around identity and injustice—and instead, speak plainly so we all know exactly what we're talking about and working to address.

We strongly encourage rereading the key terms pages out loud, if that's possible for you. The act of wrapping your mouth around these words will help shift these phrases from interesting intellectual concepts on a page to precise language that you can regularly use in order to help you in your quest to better tell the truth about the realities of inequity and hiring, plus what you plan to do about it.

Preferences for whiteness and masculinity; racism, sexism, and gender violence; white supremacy; and White Nationalism are embedded in every level of every structure, system, and relationship in the United States. This is hurtful, insidious, and at this point predictable. That's the world we live in. It's depressing, it's distressing—and it's fixable. How do we know? Because these structures were designed. We can design a new way. It will not be easy. But we refuse to give up by succumbing to overwhelm. Revolutionizing the way we treat whole people and whole peoples is possible.

This was *not* a fun list to write. We bet it was not a picnic for you to read. Thank you for reading it anyway. These terms and phrases are an important foundation for our deepened and growing understanding of what we can do and how we'll need to do it in order to transform.

When we face hard truths, when we acknowledge these painful realities together, then we can make progress toward charting a new and better course!

The Hiring Revolution alone does not upend these realities in all aspects of life. We know that. It can, however, dismantle one stronghold of these insidious forces: namely, who gets which jobs. **The Hiring Revolution is an opportunity to level the playing field in a historically racist, sexist, out-of-balance economy.**

If you're new to some or all of these concepts, or to saying or using these words or phrases at work, in this way, and with this level of specificity, welcome! We're very glad you're here! We can choose to practice consistent truth-telling together.

PART I

HOW
BAD
IS IT?

REALLY F@*#ING BAD!

STATUS-QUO HIRING FAILS JOB SEEKERS + BUSINESSES

Why we are recommending a revolution? Why aren't smart and strategic adjustments here and there in the hiring process good enough? We're glad you're thinking about this. Here's the deal: as we set out to grab the best research on workplaces and disparities for our book, we got even more worked up. Why? Because the barriers People of Color, women, and trans folks face in the workforce are stunning. And not in a good way. More like a "bury your head in a pillow and scream" kinda way.

As business owners, we know that we are engaged in a daily practice of cost-benefit analysis. Is now a good time? Should we spend money on that? Is she best for that project? We weigh the pros and the cons. We consider the real and present creative constraints (including client expectations, cash on hand, and talent on staff). Without exception, every time we learned about one of these workplace disparity statistics, it steeled our resolve to forge ahead with our revolution.

Part I of this book will help you become intimately familiar with the predictable patterns in traditional hiring that continue to prefer white men for jobs that all sorts of people could do—and do well! It paints a clear picture of exactly how intent and impact have gotten so out of alignment as we attempt to diversify our hiring practices. At a detailed level, we will review precisely how current hiring practices negatively impact the health, wealth, and overall success of People of Color, women, and trans people as they attempt to onboard into the modern workforce.

As you begin to absorb the substance of this book, we imagine you might be wondering things such as:

How am I gonna get my boss to approve such a drastic change in our process?
Surely things have gotten so much better, even in my lifetime, haven't they?!
That's outrageous! That can't possibly be true!

We get it. It's hard to read. Take our word for it: it's even harder to live.

As you turn the pages, you will be invited to confront your own experiences of being passed over for a job, making snap judgements about job candidates, and speaking up or not when something felt out of line. As you learn the facts we are about to share with you—how racism and sexism have been baked in at every level of hiring—please keep breathing. It's a lot. But as champions for change, we know you can handle it. You're not alone. We're right here with you.

CHAPTER 1

AN UGLY PICTURE
OF OUTCOMES

Here's a riddle for you: A man and his son are in a terrible accident and are rushed to the hospital in critical care. The doctor looks at the boy and exclaims, "I can't operate on this boy! He's my son!" *How can this be?*

We're not great at riddles, so there's not a ton of pressure here. But we encourage you to really try. Read it again. *What are you thinking? What's coming up?* The doctor could be his mom, other dad, etc.

If you're reading this book, we probably don't need to convince you that discrimination is a problem in the workplace. The extent of the problem, however, is staggering.

From the time you were a little kid, who have you pictured in your mind's eye when someone says "doctor"? What gender? What race? The trick in this riddle hinges on the entrenched sexist assumption that doctors are men. It's not too much of a stretch to suggest that the mental picture of that generic doctor was likely also white. And before you say, "I didn't imagine them being any particular race," let's be clear: yes, you did. Even if the features weren't clear or fully in focus, you imagined a human figure with visible skin, and that skin had a color. In a pinch, we humans tend to fill in the images of people to be like ourselves and the people we know (such as a current doctor, if you have one).

A lot of mental gymnastics take place when we imagine who this new potential colleague will be. From childhood through to today, our programming about who is and isn't likely to have a particular job permeates our psyche, and therefore every aspect of our hiring processes, with deeply harmful outcomes.

HIRING IN THE USA IS STRUCTURALLY BIASED

Full stop. P-e-r-i-o-d! Our structures give preference to white people and men.

How are we so certain? Because the people who occupy white-collar jobs in the US do not, and have not ever, accurately reflected the reality of the diversity of the United States population (across all the demographic categories listed in our Embodied Identity House).[1]

That's not just a problem because our staff photos appear super monotonous. **It's bad for business.** In the 2020 report *Diversity Wins*, McKinsey noted that "the most diverse companies are now more likely than ever to outperform less diverse peers on profitability." Based on a data set drawn from fifteen countries and more than a thousand large companies, the report—the third in a series—showed "not only that the business case remains robust but also that the relationship between diversity on executive teams and the likelihood of financial outperformance has strengthened over time." The report continued:

> *Our 2019 analysis finds that companies in the top quartile for gender diversity on executive teams were 25 percent more likely to have above-average profitability than companies in the fourth quartile—up from 21 percent in 2017 and 15 percent in 2014.*
>
> *Moreover, we found that the greater the representation, the higher the likelihood of outperformance. Companies with more than 30 percent women executives were more likely to outperform companies where this percentage ranged from 10 to 30, and in turn these companies were more likely to outperform those with even fewer women executives, or none at all. A substantial differential likelihood of outperformance—48 percent—separates the most from the least gender-diverse companies.*
>
> *In the case of ethnic and cultural diversity, our business-case findings are equally compelling: in 2019, top-quartile companies outperformed those in the fourth one by 36 percent in profitability, slightly up from 33 percent in 2017 and 35 percent in 2014. As we*

---

1   Michael Gee, "Why Aren't Black Employees Getting More White-Collar Jobs?," *Harvard Business Review*, February 28, 2018, https://hbr.org/2018/02/why-arent-black-employees-getting-more-white-collar-jobs.

have previously found, the likelihood of outperformance continues to be higher for diversity in ethnicity than for gender."[2]

Today, C-suites, boards of directors and trustees, and leaders of Fortune 500 companies are majority white and majority men.[3] But half of the people on this planet are women.[4] According to the Brookings Institution, the US population will soon be majority People of Color.[5] The shift away from white demographic dominance is already true for US children, with kids of color making up the majority of the country's 74 million youth as of the middle of 2020.[6] And since 2015, a trend has now turned into a reliable pattern: more women are graduating from US four-year colleges than men.[7]

When we habitually hire the same kinds of people over and over and over again, our companies and organizations miss out on the breadth and depth of talent, skills, experience, innovation, networks, relationships, and creativity available. Homogenous workforces lose touch with the market for their products and services, leaving openings for hungry new competitors.

DEEP DISPARITIES

When our hiring process filters out people who don't fit our image of an ideal attractive job candidate, we are living out the assumptions that have been drilled into us about who is and is not "suited" to particular sectors, companies,

2   Sundiatu Dixon-Fyle et al., "Diversity Wins: How Inclusion Matters," *McKinsey & Company*, May 19, 2020, https://www.mckinsey.com/featured-insights/diversity-and-inclusion/diversity-wins-how-inclusion-matters.

3   Susan E. Reed, "Corporate Boards Are Diversifying. The C-Suite Isn't," *Washington Post*, January 4, 2019, https://www.washingtonpost.com/outlook/corporate-boards-are-diversifying-the-c-suite-isnt/2019/01/04/c45c3328-0f02-11e9-8938-5898adc28fa2_story.html.

4   Hannah Ritchie and Max Roser, "Gender Ratio," Our World in Data, June 2019, https://ourworldindata.org/gender-ratio#:~:text=The%20sex%20ratio%20%E2%80%93%20the%20share,in%20the%20world%20was%2049.6%25.

5   William H. Frey, "The US Will Become 'Minority White' in 2045, Census Projects," Brookings, March 14, 2018, https://www.brookings.edu/blog/the-avenue/2018/03/14/the-us-will-become-minority-White-in-2045-census-projects/.

6   Rogelio Sáenz and Dudley L. Poston Jr., "Children of Color Projected to Be Majority of U.S. Youth This Year," January 9, 2020, https://www.pbs.org/newshour/nation/children-of-color-projected-to-be-majority-of-u-s-youth-this-year.

7   Alana Semuels, "Poor Girls Are Leaving Their Brothers Behind," *Atlantic*, November 27, 2017, https://www.theatlantic.com/business/archive/2017/11/gender-education-gap/546677/.

jobs, and roles. We call bulls*#t! Preferencing white and male job candidates over all other people exacerbates the health, wealth, and lifetime disparities experienced across lines of race and gender in this country.

Well-documented disparities include:

Resumé Racism

There has been more than one exposé about how different job applicants end up in the yes/maybe/no piles based on the assumptions made about them via their materials.

> According to Harvard Business School, job candidates of color who "whiten" their resumés get more interviews: "Companies are **more than twice as likely** to call minority applicants for interviews if they submit whitened résumés than [they are to call] candidates who reveal their race—and this discriminatory practice is just as strong for businesses that claim to value diversity as those that don't."[8]

Different racial groups whiten resumés in different ways, including changing names to something that reads as more "American" and/or "white sounding." Some students in the study left off major accomplishments and club affiliations for fear it would give away their racial identity and decrease their chances of getting an interview. It's heartbreaking to recognize that they are correct in that thinking.

But surely, things must be steadily improving over time?

No, ma'am! We wish they were. But nope. Evidence from a major 2017 study of racial hiring discrimination produced very troubling results. Interested to learn whether racism in hiring had decreased in the United States in recent decades, researchers from Northwestern University, Harvard, and the Institute for Social Research in Norway meticulously analyzed every available field experiment on hiring discrimination conducted from 1989 through 2015 and considered the data gathered from more than 55,000 applications submitted for more than 26,000 positions. Their findings?

---

8   Dina Gerdeman, "Minorities Who 'Whiten' Job Resumes Get More Interviews," Harvard Business School Working Knowledge, May 17, 2017, https://hbswk.hbs.edu/item/minorities-who-Whiten-job-resumes-get-more-interviews (emphasis added).

"Since 1989, whites receive on average 36% more callbacks than African Americans, and 24% more callbacks than Latinos."

"We observe no change in the level of hiring discrimination against African Americans over the past 25 years, although we find modest evidence of a decline in discrimination against Latinos."

"The results document a striking persistence of racial discrimination in US labor markets."[9]

Uff da, as we say in Minnesota. With this data in our awareness, in part II we share more intentionally equitable alternatives to resumés and other application materials to help you interrupt this decades-long pattern.

Who Is Worth What?

A defining feature of "work" is that we get paid. If we're not getting paid, the contributions we make to our households, neighborhoods, and communities are called something else:

- *Volunteering*—in our kids' school, for a local election, to help a friend with a project
- *Doing Chores*—Many people grow up in households where their parents make it very clear: "If you live here, there are things we all do in order to make sure we have what we need."
- *Slavery*—the 244 years between 1619 and 1863 of perfectly legal, unpaid, backbreaking, soul-crushing labor

So, we can all agree that getting paid is a big deal. It's a *major* piece of the pie. And yet, with a stunning level of consistency, US workers are compensated in wildly different ways depending on the bodies they come in. The impacts of pay inequity are acute and lasting, and in a capitalist economy, they result in virtually insurmountable barriers to individual, familial, and community financial safety.

Here is some salary data that knocked our socks off:

9   Lincoln Quillian et al., "Meta-Analysis of Field Experiments Shows No Change in Racial Discrimination in Hiring Over Time," *PNAS* 114, no. 41 (October 10, 2017): 10870–75, https://www.pnas.org/content/114/41/10870.

Men's Salaries across Race

According to a 2019 report from compensation research leader PayScale, "55 years after the passage of the Civil Rights Act banned pay discrimination on the basis of race, men of color still do not receive equal pay for equal work."[10]

The Economic Policy Institute reviewed the Census Bureau report on incomes, earnings, and poverty rates for 2017. Comparing median earnings of full-time, full-year workers, it discovered that median earnings of white men were $60,388 per year, compared to median earnings of $42,076 for Black men. That's a 31 percent difference.[11]

There is a **consistent gap** in earnings between Black or African American men and white men. At this point, you will be unsurprised to learn that it is not at all new: over the past seventeen years, the gap has remained basically the same.[12]

PayScale conducted a survey to learn more about the persistence of a pervasive pay gap for men along lines of race. It revealed that for every dollar a white man earns:

- Black or African American men earn **$0.87**.
- Native American and Hispanic or Latino workers earn **$0.91**.
- Pacific Islander men earn **$0.95**.
- Asian men make **$1.15**, but when researchers held all employment characteristics equal, the rate dropped to $1.02; Asian men also have the **lowest rates of being in manager roles**.[13]

"Even as Black or African American men climb the corporate ladder, they still make less than equally qualified white men."[14]

---

10   Jackson Gruver, "Racial Wage Gap for Men," PayScale, May 7, 2019, https://www.payscale.com/data/racial-wage-gap-for-men.

11   Elise Gould, Janelle Jones, and Zane Mokhiber, "Black workers have made no progress in closing earnings gaps with white men since 2000," Economic Policy Institute, September 12, 2018, https://www.epi.org/blog/black-workers-have-made-no-progress-in-closing-earnings-gaps-with-White-men-since-2000/.

12   Gould, Jones, and Mokhiber, "Black Workers Have Made No Progress in Closing Earnings Gaps."

13   Gruver, "Racial Wage Gap for Men." It's important to note that "having a higher median salary does not mean Asian men are treated impartially at work." Employee referrals, performance reviews, promotions, pay increases, opportunity gap, and occupational segregation are all contributing factors to inequity in the workplace across race.

14   Gruver, "Racial Wage Gap for Men."

These trends span centuries, sectors, and regions. Yet when we work with professionals committed to equity, one of the most dangerous patterns we witness is the misguided notion that we must somehow be above or unaffected by these systemic tsunamis of injustice. Be very careful with this kind of thinking. Why? Because it makes us complacent. It makes us miss things that are hidden in plain sight. When we build the muscles that help us notice, with increasing regularity, how we may have fallen into habits of undervaluing and therefore undercompensating men of color, we all benefit.

Building those muscles lets us develop a more accurate perspective that asks: What might I be missing? What are the micro and macro ways these consistent and damaging disparities may be seeping into our culture and way of doing business when we hire, compensate, and promote people? Over time, am I certain or uncertain about how our differently identified employees have experienced our workplace? What do I know? What do I not know? What do I think I know? Do I really know it?

Remember, we are all swimming in the waters of white supremacy culture and male-dominant preferences. These forces are not static. New waves—telling us who to trust, who to like, who to be afraid of, who to value—crest and crash every time we look at our phones, check out the news, and open our emails.

Salaries across Gender

The Institute for Women's Policy Research (IWPR) gathers and shares evidence of the persistent gap in pay between the sexes. In a study of the gap from 1960 to 2019, researchers highlighted several facts:

> Women are almost half of the workforce. They are the sole or co-breadwinner in half of American families with children. They receive more college and graduate degrees than men. Yet, on average, women continue to earn considerably less than men. In 2018, female full-time, year-round workers made only 82 cents for every dollar earned by men, a gender wage gap of 18 percent. This commonly cited statistic may be understating the extent of pay inequality; an IWPR analysis of women's and men's earnings over 15 years found that women made just half (49 percent) of what men earned.[15]

---

15 "Pay Equity and Discrimination," About, Institute for Women's Policy Research,
    https://iwpr.org/equal-pay-about/.

What Women of Color Do (and Mostly Don't) Get Paid

When combining race and gender disparities, the mistreatment is amplified.

> According to IWPR's research, if change continues at the same slow pace as it has for the past fifty years, it will take forty years—or until **2059**—for white women to finally reach pay parity. For Women of Color, the rate of change is much, much slower. Glacial, even.
>
> - Black women will not receive equal pay for equal work until the year **2130**.
> - Hispanic/Latina/Latinx women will have to wait until **2224**.[16]

This staggeringly distant date is a stark and ever-present reminder that we are not anywhere near "on the right track" or close to the moral arc just magically bending toward justice. In order to ensure that eight more generations of US Women of Color are not trapped in work which does not not adequately value them, we must interrupt this aspect of workplace brokenness.

Decision Makers' Identities Are Homogenous

As you are working to spark a Hiring Revolution in your company, it matters very much who is in charge. The folks with the veto power, who set the direction, pick parameters, and are ultimately responsible for budget, strategy, and direction of your organization writ large, all matter quite a bit.

As we consider inequities across lines of race and gender in the workplace, consider who is and is not hired into certain roles. Which folks are considered to have leadership potential, and which are not? Who is trusted with major job responsibilities, and who is not? Who are deemed the helpers, and who are coded as the drivers?

To answer the question *How bad is it?*, let's take a closer look at how predictable inequities in hiring and promotions have resulted in stark disparities when it comes to major US organizations and who actually leads them:

---

16 "Pay Equity and Discrimination."

4/500✊ ▪ "Only **four** companies in the Fortune 500—Merck & Co., TIAA, Tapestry and Lowe's—now have a [Black] chief executive, down from seven less than a decade ago."[17]

6.6% ◗ ▪ "As of June 1 (2018), 33 of the companies on the ranking of highest-grossing firms will be led by female CEOs for the first time ever. To be sure, that sum represents a disproportionately small share of the group as a whole; just **6.6%**. But it also marks a considerable jump from last year's total of 24, or 4.8%."[18]

27/500♀ ▪ As of April 2019, "Just **27** of the CEOs of the companies on the Fortune 500 are women. Since Ursula Burns left Xerox and Geisha Williams left PG&E, none of those 27 spots are held by [Black] or Latina women."[19]

To sum up, US C-suites are diversifying at a glacial pace—it is entirely possible to hurry up!

UNDERSTANDING PROTECTED CLASSES + PERVASIVE DISCRIMINATION

Now is a good time to swing back by our Embodied Identity House. Thus far, we have clarity that race is the single biggest difference in predictable workplace discrimination (in hiring, compensation, and trust to lead). Next, we layered on gender to expand the complexity of our understanding to include the everyday impacts of race and gender on different US workers.

As we work to wrap up this chapter about the impacts of inequity, we want to once again get clear about the fact that we are all always our whole entire house. We have all these rooms, whether we are forced to pay attention to any one aspect of our identity or not.

---

17 Lauretta Charlton, "Study Examines Why Black Americans Remain Scarce in Executive Suites," *New York Times*, December 9, 2019, https://www.nytimes.com/2019/12/09/us/black-in-corporate-america-report.html.

18 Claire Zillman, "The Fortune 500 Has More Female CEOs Than Ever Before," *Fortune*, May 16, 2019, https://fortune.com/2019/05/16/fortune-500-female-ceos/.

19 Courtney Connley, "Reminder: Today Isn't Equal Pay Day for All Women," *CNBC*, April 2, 2019, https://www.cnbc.com/2018/04/10/today-isnt-equal-pay-day-for-black-latina-or-native-american-women.html744.

In order to understand how and why identity plays such a pivotal role in the struggle for equity in the workplace, it is wise to connect to the ways in which identity has been, and remains, a hot topic. It is through the lens of these multiple identities that all sorts of assumptions get made about who we are and, as workers, what people think we are and are not capable of doing, and doing well.

What are the rules? Who is protected? And why?

Identity-based workplace discrimination (including refusal to hire, pay disparities, sexual harassment, and more) has been a hot topic for policy makers and the public for the past sixty years and more. Laws that protect workers are important! In recent decades we, along with many of our friends and colleagues, have worked tirelessly to ensure comprehensive workplace discrimination protections federally, statewide, in cities, and even at the specific level of company codes of conduct. Federal and local laws protecting workers against race, gender, disability, religious, ethnic, and sexual orientation discrimination have been written, passed, and signed into law because pervasive race and gender (and other identity) **discrimination has been proven to be widespread**. From federal to local lists of who is covered under these ordinances, a variety of groups are specified in order to ensure application of said law.

The way we think about it is that nondiscrimination protections (whether they are established at the ballot box; by a city council; by a diversity, equity, and inclusion (DEI) council; or by a court) give us a backstop when workers are mistreated. But laws alone are *not sufficient* when it comes to protecting workers and promoting equitable practices.

We raise these points because we recognize that there is a policy fixation on "solving" the problems of racism and sexism in the US workplace. How does this play out? Well, it can feel way too easy to say, "That's against our rules, so that doesn't happen here." Oh, how we wish that were true!

Here's what we know: movements for equity have been formally supported by law since the Civil Rights Act of 1965. And yet, centuries of behavioral norms continue to trump the rules when it comes to day-to-day life for US workers. Identity-driven workplace discrimination was stitched into the fabric of our country's colonialist beginnings. Consider workplace discrimination in the context of the legacy of slavery and anti-Blackness in this country:

slavery + slave codes	→	reconstruction	→	no-loitering laws + uneven drug charges	→	higher rates of Black incarceration

slavery + slave codes	→	reconstruction	→	no-loitering laws + uneven drug charges	→	higher rates of Black incarceration
labor controlled by "owners"	→	certain jobs deemed "beneath" white people	→	racially imbalanced pay	→	"no felonies" hiring policies
owning class remains vast majority white	→	whiteness/ lightness seen as supremely desirable	→	behaviors associated with white people rewarded at work	→	Black + brown labor remain controlled

Our history, without question, continues to shape and influence our present experiences. When racist policy is treated as history and not acknowledged as also part of our present reality, we get tricked into believing we've magically evolved around race and gender. Unfortunately, we continue to live with near-constant false, predatory, and dehumanizing messages that white and masculine workers are supreme and more capable. And while we may not say it to ourselves explicitly, it seeps into our daily hiring practices, limiting who we imagine might take on a particular role and excel.

ASSUMPTIONS, MYTHS, STEREOTYPES, BIAS, PREJUDICE, DISCRIMINATION, HARASSMENT

To understand the impacts of inequity in hiring, it is wise to revisit the range of ways inequity can and does currently manifest.

Racism and sexism are not simply the individual acts of mean people. Cultural patterns, company norms, and notions of "acceptability" have all conspired to stack the economy against People of Color, women, and trans folks and toward white people and men.

Take a deep breath. It sucks to acknowledge this every time.

As you consider all the ways that you can be part of meaningful change in your workplace, stay conscious of this entire range of how racism and sexism sneak into our processes.

With relationship to hiring, here are examples of how each ouch can show up:

Assumption → accepted as true without proof
Example: Women aren't interested in tech.

Myth → widely held but false belief
Example: People for whom English is not a first language won't be great at customer service jobs.

Stereotype → widely held, fixed oversimplified image
Example: Gay men are gregarious and prefer roles where they get to schmooze with people.

Bias → prejudice in favor of or against as compared to another
Example: Black people make good event planners because they know the best music.

Prejudice → preconceived opinion that is not based on reason or actual experience
Example: People won't feel comfortable around a male nurse.

Discrimination → unjust treatment of different categories of people
Example: She hasn't gone to college, so she isn't qualified to complete these tasks.

Harassment → aggressive pressure or intimidation
Example: Striking a "hard bargain" during the salary negotiations is part of making a job offer—either take this or leave it.

As you continue to hone your skills of recognizing and grappling with inequities, remember that there is this whole range of behaviors and thought processes, all of which matter. Added together, these seemingly miniscule blips in our thinking and behavior stack up.

CHAPTER 2

HOW EXISTING PRACTICES
PRODUCE BAD RESULTS

Hiring Revolution invites us to carefully explore the places where our intent and impact do not match. We all have programming and preferences that shape our expectations of who belongs in different workplaces, especially our own. We all make assumptions about situations and people. It's just part of how human brains work! However, how we *react* does not have to define how we *respond*. Let's consider how and why social programming and biology influence our reactions, including in hiring, and how we can shift our responses to drive more equitable processes, including a tool we use every day: Investigate Your Instincts.

PROGRAMMING + PREFERENCES

Traits associated with whiteness and masculinity in the US have been assigned higher value and importance when it comes to all things leadership and hard work. This skewed sense of what different bodies are capable of in the workplace includes (but is not limited to): perception, assumptions, and experiences related to intellect, physical ability, leadership presence, team leadership style, motivation, drive, and more.

Yuck.

Preferences toward or away from certain types of behaviors and people are pervasive and, thus, predictable. These preferences are baked in to our psyches[1] in all areas of life: news, school, our interactions with institutions, and more. Consequently, we need to carefully examine our gut instincts about who would be the "best fit" when we're hiring. We're not saying, "Never trust your gut." We believe deeply that each of us is capable of accessing deep body wisdom. That said, our gut feelings all too often replicate racist and sexist societal patterning. Thus, we've got to be careful.

Years ago, our friend and colleague Anil Hurkadli taught us the phrase *Investigate Your Instincts*.

> *Trina:* As a white girl growing up in the Midwest in the 1980s, I remember the evening news being on in the background while my dad made dinner, and the car radio being on while my mom was driving me to softball practice or my grandparents' for a visit. I was just a little kid: I was only ever half listening, and yet to this day, I can recall the barrage of bad news flowing through the airwaves and into my little ears. I was being told over and over and over again what to be afraid of and who to be afraid of: strangers in cars, drugs, Halloween candy, men, Black men, immigrant men, Muslim men, people from other countries, and more.

F*#k. Programming happening in the background of our lives is *not* benign.

> *Trina:* My teachers looked like me. My coaches looked like my dad. And I was trying to figure out, in my body, how I did and didn't fit in. What I was and wasn't expected to do. Who I was and wasn't supposed to be around. And what was scary and what was safe.

The cultural pattern of racially skewed reporting is so pervasive that local activists, organizers, and journalists have called attention to the different ways that gun violence is reported based on whether or not the shooter was a Person of Color or a white person.[2] People of Color are described as "terrorists" acting

---

1   Douglas Starr, "Meet the Psychologist Exploring Unconscious Bias—and Its Tragic Consequences for Society," *Science*, March 26, 2020, https://www.sciencemag.org/news/2020/03/meet-psychologist-exploring-unconscious-bias-and-its-tragic-consequences-society.

2   For example, see Alexandra Bell, "Counternarratives," Public Work, Alexandra Bell http://www.alexandrabell.com/public-work.

on behalf of their entire race, religion, or country of origin. White men who shoot up movie theaters, schools, synagogues, and shopping centers are described as "lone wolves" who likely had "mental health problems" for which they should have received treatment.[3] To be clear: gun violence is HORRIBLE, no matter who shoots whom. That said, this extreme example illustrates the ways in which what and who we fear is due, in very large part, to the barrage of messaging coming our way.

Very heavy sigh.

This brings us back to "likability," "fit," and the gut feelings we experience throughout hiring and interview processes. *We have all been programmed, and we all have preferences.* These impact how we feel about who would and wouldn't be a good fit on our teams at work. We might even go so far as to convince ourselves we were doing a job candidate a favor by not hiring them because they probably wouldn't like working with us all that much.

Uh-oh!

Here's the deal:
- Programming just is. None of us is immune. It's about what we, as adults, do with the programming that matters.
- We have all been race and gender programmed, whether it's in our everyday awareness or not.
- We have each been rewarded and punished for our behaviors based on the expectations put upon us by family, community, and work.

This programming influences and determines what has been coded as "professional," "ideal," and "impressive" in the context of hiring.

Some of us grew up in an economic class context that presented the opportunity to learn how to perform preferred white and masculine behaviors, such as what to wear, how to talk, and which credentials to get in order to be taken seriously. We don't want to assume here that learning how to practice whiteness and masculinity is a desirable goal for all people with class privilege; rather, we are naming a way in which economic privilege creates access to

---

3   Annalisa Merelli, "'Lone Wolf' vs 'Terrorist': The Vocabulary of Mass Shootings," *Quartz*, October 2, 2017, https://qz.com/1092042/las-vegas-shooting-terrorist-vs-lone-wolf/.

whiteness and masculinity as leadership qualities. The challenge then becomes to unpack whether we are consciously using these tools at work, performing them to get along, or subconsciously assimilating and losing our sense of self.

> *Alfonso:* I can still remember going to work with my white dad
> on "bring your child to work day" and hearing and seeing how
> he spoke and operated in particular ways in the office that he
> definitely didn't at home. I knew he was the same person, but it was
> like seeing "work dad" versus "home dad." When I got my first job
> many years later, I remember actively considering how I was going
> to be similar and different to him because my colleagues saw my
> dark eyes, dark hair, and brown skin.

Problems and prejudice arise whenever we are not paying attention to our own race and gender programming at work.

Assumptions, myth, bias, and stereotypes are like a song playing in the background of our lives: ever present, sometimes quiet, but shaping the silence nonetheless. For example, one predominant myth spoon-fed to white workers is that each white person gets to be a singular, special snowflake, while People of Color are treated as representative of an entire race of people, whether in redemptive or embarrassing ways. It's ridiculous! For example, when a white kid screws up and it makes the news, that kid is described as "troubled." When a kid of color messes up in a similar way, we are bombarded with statistics about that neighborhood's crime rates and the presence of a whole racial or ethnic group.

Your job is to start noticing how similar behavior is discussed in very different ways depending on the bodies engaging in the behavior. Building this capacity will help you catch the same problematic narratives while you hire.

ASSUMPTIONS IN ACTION

Imagine that you're interviewing. A six-foot-four Black man walks through your door, shakes your hand, and takes his seat.

Take a breath, in through your nose and out through your mouth. Close your eyes if it helps. What are your first thoughts? Reactions? Wonderings? Assumptions?

Next, imagine that a five-foot-five white woman walks through your door, shakes your hand, and takes her seat.

Take another breath. What are your first thoughts? Reactions? Wonderings? Assumptions?

This is an uncomfortable exercise. We get that. Stick with us.

- What's your comfort level in the first minute of being around each of these people?
- How similar or different is each candidate to current relationships you have in your life?
- How similar or different is each candidate to current relationships you have at work?

Be honest. Let's Investigate Your Instincts.

> *Trina:* Let's get "mean girl" about this for a minute—a process that helps me Investigate My Instincts by helping me be more honest. If I were a mean girl (which, sometimes, I still am), here are the thoughts that would pass through my head and the sensations I would notice in my body, in rapid succession, in no particular order:

A six-foot-four Black man walks through your door, shakes your hand, and takes his seat.

- My inner dialogue: "Jesus, he's tall! How tall is he? I wonder if he played basketball. I don't notice a wedding ring. His résumé says he graduated from college in 2003, but 'Black don't crack,' right? Oh shit, as a white person, I should not be thinking things like that. I wonder if he's been to jail. What's with the gap in his employment history?"
- My body sensations: He's physically intimidating and I'm certain he could overpower me, so I'm going to sit up tall, pitched forward, shoulders back, appearing my full strength. Also, I purposefully won't shut the door all the way so we're not alone without other folks being able to hear me.

**A five-foot-five white woman walks through your door,
shakes your hand, and takes her seat.**

- My inner dialogue: "She seems nice. I like her hair. Oh, her earrings are cute too! I wonder if she needs those glasses or if they are for show to make her appear smart during interviews. Hmmmm, her voice is higher than I thought it would be. I wonder if Doug thinks she's attractive. Her laugh is a little irritating. Her engagement ring—I don't see a wedding band—is really big. I wonder what her fiancé does for a living and if she even needs this job? I wonder if she'll want to take time off for a wedding or kids or both?"

- My body sensations: I don't love that she's skinnier than me. I wish I could wear a pencil skirt like that. I have been around a lot of girls who look like her. It would be fine if I had to leave for a second to use the restroom during this interview, I get her, I'll be right back.

It is very embarrassing to share that I've had all those thoughts at one point or another while interviewing job candidates. It feels awful to acknowledge that to myself and to you. Feeling this way is normal—it's a process of waking up to that which we've been asleep to all these years. The value of investigating these instincts is that I learn more about myself and can start to actively counter my preprogrammed myths and value judgments.

Human brains are wild: we can think all those things in rapid succession while also asking questions, listening, and taking notes as part of the hiring process. Whoa!

Now it's your turn. If the first time around you thought general things like, "I'd just be curious about each candidate!" or, "I approach all job candidates the same!", we invite you to go deeper.

ACTIVITY—INITIAL IMPRESSIONS

Reread the candidate descriptions and take stock of your inner dialogue and your body sensations. Make your best guesses about how you would react.

Then consider: what did your instincts tell you about each candidate and whether or not you would like working with them? How do you feel after surfacing likely reactions? Does your inner dialogue match your espoused goals and values? Anything else arising you want to jot down so you're sure to remember it later?

a. He might be intimidating, it might be harder to work with him because I'm so different from him. I would be walking on eggshells and focusing on not saying the wrong thing all the time. There's more weight behind ~~navi~~ a white person and a Black person working together. He might have family or life stuff that could get in the way of work.

b. I feel bad about most of this. Some of it comes from me not wanting to cause harm to a person of color ~~and~~ but otherwise my reactions are not representative of my values.

BIAS + BRAIN SCIENCE

Here's the thing: as humans, we are still animals. Biologically, we are wired to sort.[4] This sorting is a character trait of our evolutionary desire to stay alive. Our animal instincts are scanning for danger and safety *all the time*, whether we want them to be doing that or not. When our neurotransmitters are experiencing something new, the first thing we're trying to do is make sense of it.

Who are you?

What are you? (People ask "racially ambiguous" and gender-nonconforming folks that all the time—strangers! It's wild!)

Who are you to me?

What should I do to protect myself—right now and into the future?

Even those of us who fancy ourselves curious have an initial reaction to differences (like a woman coming into a job interview wearing a head covering): we filter this information as either a threat or not.

COMFORT IS NOT THE SAME THING AS SAFETY

When it comes to interacting with job candidates, colleagues, and even strangers on the street who seem different than us in a way that feels like it matters (like race rather than left-handedness, for example), *our millennia-old instincts fixate on staying alive and thus go into hyperdrive, often conflating "this feels uncomfortable" with "this feels unsafe."* Wanting to make everyone comfortable is an unattainable goal that our clients ask about regularly. Real talk: even we're not comfortable right now, and we write and teach about race and gender discrimination for a living!

> *Alfonso:* I learned a long time ago from my friend and mentor Susan Raffo that **discomfort is simply our body's reaction to new information**.

Thus, if we are interviewing a job candidate who is unlike the workers we already have on our team or at our company (older or younger, darker or lighter, speaks with an accent or doesn't, wears a headwrap or Star of David, is gender nonconforming), we might catch ourselves almost immediately

---

4   Mahzarin Banaji and Anthony Greenwald, *Blindspot* (New York: Delacorte, 2013).

wondering about how comfortable or uncomfortable everyone would be working together. The uneasy feeling that arises when you consider hiring the first or only woman, Person of Color, Jewish person, and so on is important to note. If your gut is telling you, "They just don't feel like they'd be an ideal fit" and/or a different candidate really does "feel right," your internal racial and gender biases are showing up loud. That's new information! You don't want to be feeling this, but being able to recognize that you *are* feeling it is new information you can act on to the contrary.

If your goal is to transform the workforce and the economy toward racial and gender equity, the candidates you meet and choose, and the process you participate in, won't "fit" or "feel" like what you've done before. Genuinely considering new kinds of people to fill the jobs you have will be loaded with discomfort, especially at first, because you are upending the status quo.

It's worth it! We promise!

Re-Actions vs. Responses

One of our mentors, Debra Peevey, who also serves as the lead Enneagram coach to the employees in our company, taught us years ago about the important distinction between re-actions and responses. You are probably thinking we messed up in our spell check. We didn't. Deb taught us that re-acting is exactly that: you are re-acting, doing something you've already done for the second, third, fourth, or even three-thousandth time. The shorthand she taught us for catching it is to notice when something is giving us "the stale taste of the familiar." As in, "We have had this exact fight already," "We keep getting stuck at the same point of the puzzle," "I'm irritated by that exact behavior you're doing again." Get it? Cool.

At work, we want to continue to feel forward movement—actually tackling and dealing with one problem after another. Moving on. Getting further. Not relitigating the same grievances over and over again.

Here's that neuroscience again: you know now that we are all mostly unaware of how thoughts, feelings, and sensations course through our bodies at near lightning speed. What we discern from our body and brain bouncing like a pinball between fight, flight, and freeze is, in general, a comfy or yucky feeling. Think about how you feel:

- when you meet someone
- when you are engaged in deep work with someone
- when you are standing at an ATM and somebody gets in line behind you

Does your face get flushed? Do you get goose bumps? Does the hair on the back of your neck stand up?

> *Trina:* Here's what's weird about how all those physical responses have been influenced by the racism and sexism I have experienced. My body tenses up if/when I notice a man of color behind me in line. My body hardly even notices if a woman of any race ends up physically close or near to me. I have been conditioned by the whole wide world to fear men of color. Oooof, this stuff runs deep.

So, what's the takeaway?
We **can't** control our body's **re-actions** to the biases we've ingested, but We **can** control our **responses**.
As adults we possess both the capacity and responsibility to behave in ways that align with our most deeply held values.
When it comes to hiring, instinctive pattern matching means that people who make hiring decisions in the United States very consistently choose the dominant—therefore the most familiar and, dare we say, "comfortable"—characteristics of whiteness and masculinity. That's how we keep ending up with companies and leadership more homogenous than the nation itself.
In order to slow down and catch ourselves inside an instinct moment, we offer this approach to help you slow down and properly Investigate Your Instincts.

ACTIVITY—RE-ACTIONS

A) Imagine you're interviewing a job candidate: What is the inbound information that is coming your way? (Take notes here or in a notebook.)

- *With the senses currently available to you, what do you think you hear? smell? see? taste? touch?*
- *What did you read? Who is the source? Why do you trust this information?*
- *Practice writing down all that is inbound.*

B) How are you re-acting? (We hyphenate on purpose here—to remind you that re-acting means acting in a way that you have acted before.) Think of re-actions and re-activity as instinctual—like blinking, flinching, or having the hair on the back of your neck stand up.

- *What sensations is your body having? (e.g., tingly, warm, clenched)*
- *What is your innermost dialogue?*
- *How are you noticing your body and/or mind moving toward a decision/ something to do because of how you are re-acting?*
- *In what ways can you imagine your instinctual re-actions being programmed by your voluminous experiences with bias? (For example, how do you find yourself re-acting when a woman gets onto an elevator with you compared to a man doing the same thing? What about a white person standing behind you at an ATM? And now a Black person?)*
- *What do you know? Are you certain? What are you assuming? What don't you know yet?*
- *Practice writing down your re-actions.*

C) Now, after making sense of the inbound information and wrestling with your variety of re-actions, what is the values-aligned response you are consciously choosing?

- *What can you do to move from subconscious re-acting to conscious choice making?*
- *How will you ensure that your responses, how you ultimately choose to behave, are aligned with your values?*
- *What will you do to reach your race and gender diversity goals for your team as you make decisions about how you will respond?*
- *How have you made sure you have considered a wide range of choices available—breaking away from limited, binary thinking?*
- *What could support you to interrupt programmed behavior that preferences whiteness and masculinity?*
- *What questions should you ask next?*
- *What could you try?*

INTENT VS. IMPACT

We start from the assumption that people are *not* intentionally allowing their preferences for whiteness and masculinity to take hold when they hire. Biases are sneaky: they pop up at times and in ways we least expect. **What's important is to recognize and take responsibility for the ways in which our intentions in hiring have not always resulted in the impacts we wanted.**

Justifying the outcome you've contributed to by describing what you had *intended* to do is futile. You are an adult. You did damage. You now have the opportunity to take responsibility, make amends, and pivot to a next, better action. No question, this sounds easier in writing than it is to practice in real life. We get that! Nevertheless, we implore you to stay out of "intent justification" and instead focus your precious attention on "impact inquiry." Basically, no matter what you were *trying* to do, this is the actual result.

How do you feel about that?

Was it close to or far away from what you most wished would happen?

We often ask our clients, "So, now what?" It's a real question: So, _____ happened. Based on that truth, now what?

DROP THE MYTHS OF FAIRNESS, OBJECTIVITY, AND COLOR BLINDNESS IN HIRING PROCESSES

What myths do we need to jettison in order to live out the Hiring Revolution?

As a reminder, myths are *widely held* but are *false beliefs*.

Stop. Take a real, deep breath. The three myths we're about to discuss are deeply ingrained, to the point that you may have believed one or more of them as facts right up until you were today years old. You might not like us for a few minutes after we tell you to let them go in order to be equitable in hiring. We get that. And it's important. So we're going to keep telling you the truth, even if it means you argue with us for a bit.

- Fairness is **not a good goal**.
- Objectivity is **not a real thing**.
- Color blindness is **impossible**.

RE: Fairness

In the United States, we are not now and never have been **born onto a level playing field**. White people are preferred. White wealth is developed and passed down from generation to generation. The institutions that make up our country's ecosystem and infrastructure, including schools, banks, hospitals, and workplaces, all produce consistently better results for white people. When we acknowledge the pervasive and structural impact of racism, misogyny, and homophobia, it behooves us to consider how we can level the playing field throughout each part of our hiring processes.

Why? Equality versus equity. Equality is the Pollyanna belief that if we treat everyone exactly the same way, then we are being "fair."

Not so.

Equity is the emergent understanding that because we do *not* start on a level playing field, and because we are each all the rooms of our whole Embodied Identity House, we will each need distinct resources in order to be successful.

Tyrai Bronson-Pruitt, our friend and colleague, describes the important distinctions between equality and equity in Team Dynamics' trainings this way:

> *Imagine you found out that people in a town didn't have shoes. Good news! You have access to hundreds of pairs of shoes! You want to be fair, so you develop and execute a plan to send 256 pairs of size 8 women's shoes to this town. Yay!*
>
> *Right?*
>
> *Or no?*
>
> *What's the problem?*
>
> *1: After noticing the people in this town didn't have shoes, did you ask if they needed or wanted shoes?*
>
> *2: If yes, did you learn about the sizes and shapes and styles of shoes people might need in order to wear these shoes successfully (for example, I can't have a high heel, I have wide feet, I need my shoes to be waterproof)?*

An oversimplification, to be sure. But it gets the point across. Equity recognizes that different people will need different things in order to participate equally and asks those people—and listens to them about—what they need.

"Fair" treatment does not mean identical treatment.

Have you ever sat on a committee responsible for hiring and experienced things such as these?

- "As long as we're fair about which resumés end up in the 'yes' pile."
- "When comparing and contrasting these candidates' qualifications, the fair thing to do is offer the job to candidate X because he has the most experience."
- "It wouldn't be fair to ask that candidate a follow-up question during the interview because we didn't do that with any other candidates."

Do you want some level of consistency in your hiring process? Definitely! But talking to and treating your job candidates identically will result in the preference of humans with the most access to resources (including health, technology, mentors, and time) in your process.

RE: Objectivity

Hiring is not objective. **Hiring is one of the most subjective decisions you will ever make.** You are comparing and contrasting capable adults based on myriad criteria and a rubric that creates a false hierarchy rather than a web of top talent. Each of your qualified candidates would bring something unique to this role and your organization because of the lived experience they have had right up until coming through your doors. You are not comparing and contrasting apples and oranges. A more apt analogy would be comparing apples and skyscrapers!

Most hiring processes identify a bunch of adults who all *could* do the job. Who *is* going to do the job?

Imagine that your final candidate pool includes:

A) a white man in his midthirties with a relevant four-year degree and access to his own car
B) a woman of Filipino descent in her late fifties with twenty years' relevant job experience who currently lives ninety minutes from your office

C) a racially ambiguous (to you) early-twenty-something person who is self-taught and currently makes their living between three different "side hustles" as a freelancer

These three people have all made it to your final candidate pool, so they are qualified to do the job. Yet they are wildly different from one another. There is no such thing as one "objectively" better or best candidate. There are simply concurrent realities of how different people got prepared differently for a role such as this.

We diminish our processes by pretending to have objectivity when it comes to who we want on our teams at work. Instead, think about what an incredible opportunity it is to talk to qualified people and determine who meets your needs, given your goals.

RE: Color Blindness

In an article published in June 2020 in *Oprah Magazine*, Samantha Vincenty interviewed two experts on color-blind ideology, sociologists Eduardo Bonilla-Silva, author of *Racism without Racists*, and Meghan Burke, author of *Colorblind Racism*. Both were crystal clear that while the notion of color-blind thinking emerged with good intent, it has had really problematic results. In the interview, Burke notes, "It borrows right from that last third of Martin Luther King Jr.'s speech, where he says that he wants people to see his kids for the content of their character, not the color of their skin. So I think it's easy for a lot of well-meaning white folks to hear that and say, 'Well, gosh, okay. Yeah. I don't want that to be the primary lens that I use to judge people's character.'"

Burke also points to US individualism, our collective and historic emphasis on independence and self-reliance as principles, as a contributing factor. If health problems, poverty, and other problems are routinely described as personal moral failings, responsibility for overcoming them falls on the individual, rather than on the broken structures of which they are symptoms. Burke summarizes it as, "If you do the right thing, you'll be successful. If you don't, it's your fault."[5]

---

5   Samantha Vincenty, "Being 'Color Blind' Doesn't Make You Not Racist—In Fact, It Can Mean the Opposite," *Oprah Magazine*, June 12, 2020, https://www.oprahmag.com/life/relationships-love/a32824297/color-blind-myth-racism/.

The truth is, we absolutely do experience color. All of us. All the time. It's hard to admit, and while we'd like to think that color has no impact on how we feel or how we act, it does shape our actions.

What you can do:

1. When you come into contact with color-blind rhetoric (or even catch yourself engaging in it), remind your hiring committee that while the job candidates you are considering are all individuals, their access to opportunities and experiences has been influenced by their mix of identities throughout their lives.

2. Talk about race and color as present and relevant consistently. Too often, deferring to a color-blind mindset shuts down conversations about the relevance of race and racism by essentially declaring the conversation closed.

3. Don't fall for any version of the "pull yourselves up by your bootstraps" or "special hero" narratives that breed an "against all odds, they rose, and so could everyone else if they try hard enough" kind of racially color-blind nostalgia. You can marvel at exceptional people and still remember that the very large structures at play continue to raise insurmountable barriers for folks who are smart, capable, ambitious, and motivated.

THE LIKABILITY TRAP—HOW OUR PREFERENCES INFORM WHICH JOB CANDIDATES FEEL BEST TO US

Think about a memorable experience you had as an interviewer. Maybe you liked how someone shook hands: not too hard, not too soft, not too much up and down, not hanging on too long. Or perhaps a story they shared about a challenge they'd overcome resonated with you. You may have even felt compelled by or appreciative of their perfume or cologne—smell is a really powerful sense! But what does likability actually mean in hiring?

Trina: Yesterday I was on the phone with a Team Dynamics client, and we got to talking about how hiring committees discuss what they just experienced in conducting interviews. If you were eavesdropping, you'd hear such things as:

- *"What I especially liked about him was . . ."*
- *"I didn't feel good when she . . ."*
- *"I loved how he talked about . . ."*

That is, essentializing whole people into how much we liked them, or not. Likability. What does it mean? And why is it a problem in hiring? Many of us are operating from an impossible expectation that: (A) we must be liked by everyone we work with, and (B) we must like everyone we work with.

If we don't, we fear that we cannot enjoy ourselves, we are not maximally productive, and our workplaces cannot thrive. Untrue.

We call bulls*#t on likability as a hiring criteria. Many of us are not particularly capable of liking people we don't yet know. In a hiring process, we're basing that feeling on shockingly few data points. Further, data on how much we like someone seldom has much to do with their ability to do the work, participate on a team, and create whatever it is we create as a company.

So, what does likability have to do with all this?

We trust our instincts regarding who we like and don't like at first meeting. But, as we explored earlier, our instincts have been impacted by years of programming. Our experiences of liking or disliking, loving, or despising people who have character traits similar to the person we are interviewing inevitably shape our impressions of candidates as they interview.

For example, if an interviewee reminds you of your brother's best friend, and you really liked that guy, you might feel immediate indicators of comfort around him. But if your brother's best friend was a pain in the ass who had no manners at your aunt's dinner table and who once walked in on you in the bathroom during a sleepover, it might take you some time to warm up.

ACTIVITY—PREFERENCE CHECK
Pause + Reflect

Be honest! There are no bonus points for the most polite answers.

What characteristics or qualities do you find *likeable* in other people?	What are the characteristics of a person you feel most *comfortable* around?
Imagine that optimally *likeable* person. What is their age, race, gender, physical appearance, smell, smile, and handshake style?	Imagine that person you feel *comfortable* around. What is their age, race, gender, physical appearance, smell, smile, and handshake style?

In Programming + Preferences, we discussed the influence of programming on how our instincts and preferences develop. Preferences extend to the type of people we like being in relationship with, and relationships include with whom we want to work.

Let's do a quick preference check. Set a timer for one minute and answer the twenty questions below. Yep, we need you to do it that fast! Don't worry: there is no way to fail this quiz. In fact, there won't even be scoring. Humor us. (If you don't like drawing in this book, just jot down on scrap paper the one word out of each set that you prefer.)

The question is, Who would you most like to work with or near?
You don't need a reason why. You cannot circle both. Pick one.

Set the timer for one minute.
Did you do it? Now . . . ready—steady—go!

I prefer my coworkers/colleagues/boss to be:

Fat/Heavy   or   Thin

Bald   or   Have Hair

Able Bodied   or   In a Wheelchair

(English Speaking)	or	English with an Accent (Southern, British, Spanish)
(Young)	or	Old
(Gay)	or	Straight
(Have Kids)	or	Don't Have Kids
Deaf	or	(Hearing)
(A US Citizen)	or	Not a US Citizen
Transgender	or	(Cisgender)
(Jewish)	or	Christian
Wealthy	or	(Working Class)
(Have a Car)	or	Don't Have a Car
Pregnant	or	(Not Pregnant)
Muslim	or	(Atheist)
(Tall)	or	Short
Fast Talker	or	(Slow Talker)
Introvert	or	(Extrovert)
Loud	or	(Soft-spoken)
Hugger	or	(Handshaker)

Okay, stop.

Take three deep breaths, each one deeper than the last.

Take your time. Really breathe. Resist the urge to leave your body. Stay in it.

Keep breathing as you now take some time to review your list of selected preferences.

Now let's do some freewriting to figure out what you notice and what you can learn from your reactions.

Read back over your circled responses:

How did that feel? What are your initial reflections on your own reactions?

Where did you get stuck choosing one answer? And where did you fly through answering?

What do you notice about your preferences being similar to and different from the ways that you yourself behave, are, or act?

How have these preferences shown up in how you behave at work in your past?

How do you imagine your preferences showing up when you hire?

How might these preferences be limiting your desire and/or ability to build a kickass team full of people good at all sorts of different and complementary things?

Last question on likability: What has been the impact of your criteria for likeable and comfortable?

- I feel like some of these would be different day to day ???
- It looks like I prefer a lot of traits that I relate to, which are more often aligned w/ privilege
- I got stuck on many of them - size, pregnant/not, car ownership, english speaking/US citizen, introvert/extrovert
- in the past I have experienced good working relationships w/ people who I related to on a personal level and identities are deeply connected to that
- I feel like my impression of someone's work abilities is definitly tied to how well I think I would communicate with them

Self-awareness work can clarify preferences for whiteness and masculinity that will show up in hiring. For example, here are Alfonso's answers:

> If I'm honest with myself, here's who my most *likeable* person is:
> A white woman,
> near my age,
> who smiles after every response,
> has a "smart" outfit on,
> and manages to work in a pop culture reference in her responses.
>
> My *comfortable* person?
> An effeminate man,
> what some would call stereotypically gay,
> my age or
> younger.

What has been the impact? I have hired many "nice" white women in their thirties and have had a number of interns and staff who are gay men younger than me. These aren't bad people; in fact, they are smart, strategic, and very capable people. However, **my overreliance on what has felt likeable or comfortable means I didn't end up building the team I wanted across race and gender**. I was missing perspectives and ultimately built teams that reinforced singular ways of thinking and doing. I haven't stopped hiring white women or gay men, but I now pause and think, *Am I drawn to this candidate because they are likeable or comfortable to me? Or am I drawn to them because they are adding a perspective we don't have on our team already?*

You get the point. Our preferences run deep.

- Who do we like?
- Who do we feel comfortable around?
- Who has characteristics or mannerisms that we recognize and understand versus those that we don't?

When we say we value and are seeking a diverse workplace, we must first recognize that our mean-girl habits likely didn't die in middle school. In insidious ways, that can stay hidden unless we do our work; we might still be as judgy as we were about who did and didn't belong at our table in the cafeteria. Let's grow up. Let's wake up. Let's Investigate Your Instincts and, through all that noise, clear paths to compare and contrast job candidates' skills, perspectives, and experiences meaningfully.

CHAPTER 3

CHOREOGRAPHING THE DANCE BETWEEN
OUR IDENTITIES

We've spoken broadly, so now it's time to engage with the current ways that racism and sexism influence how hiring happens at *your* organization.

How does your company's search and selection process implicitly and explicitly reinforce preferences for whiteness and masculinity?

That question is multifaceted and important, and it can feel hard to answer. We want to help. Let's start with this phrase: Notice, Name, and Navigate.

Notice, without assigning too much meaning initially, the patterns in your hiring processes you and your team engage in that relate to race and gender (whether you've ever considered those relationships before or not).

For example:

- When we think about "appropriate" dress for an interview, we have in our minds what men, women, and trans people who are "taking the interview seriously" would wear.
- We start talking about candidates as "diverse" if they have a name that doesn't seem white.
- We assume we will interview and select a certain gender for this role.

Name the impact of those patterns in preferencing certain job candidates over others. Acknowledge how you have assigned meaning—good and/or bad. Specifically, are those patterns viewed differently for candidates who are People of Color versus white, and for candidates who are men versus women or trans?

Using the three examples above, here is how we might name what we noticed:

- "She was showing a lot of cleavage—that didn't feel work appropriate."
- "I've never even heard of that college; I wonder if it's accredited/decent/good."
- "I bet he will end up having to take so much time off for medical emergencies and birthdays and soccer games."

Navigate the distance between your current process and where it should be to align with your company values and stated hiring goals. Consciously and explicitly compare your espoused goals with your current behaviors.

Here are examples of Notice, Name, Navigate in action:

Sexism example

Notice	Name	Navigate
When we discuss candidates who are women, we talk about how well they might fit in and with whom they would get along. When we discuss candidates who are men, we talk about their leadership presence.	The impact is that we select women based on likeability and men based on leadership qualities—both of which are not defined and neither of which has been included in a shared rubric for selection. Moreover, in these instances we are most often picking men for management roles.	We have a goal of hiring more women into management roles. This pattern of talking about different-gender candidates differently is out of alignment with our values and goals. We need to create a shared rubric for the hiring team to use and practice catching ourselves when we preference personality characteristics that feel personally comfortable or interesting.

Racism example

Notice	Name	Navigate
When names like Maria or LaShawn are on a resumé, we wonder out loud if they are "ready" for this role in comparison to names like Heather or Brian.	Are we imagining "unprofessional" or "underprepared" People of Color when we see names we don't associate with white people? Our finalist pools are predominantly white, and the kinds of names that make it through resumé screening are more often than not stereotypically white-sounding names.	We have a goal of 40 percent of finalist candidates being People of Color, and our implicit assumptions about names are resulting in a wildly imbalanced finalist pool. We need to catch ourselves assuming whole experiences based on a name when we're reviewing materials.

Gender Expression example

Notice	Name	Navigate
A person logs into Zoom for an interview, their name is Cory, and we can't tell if and how this person identifies with a gender.	I'm curious if we will feel less close to Cory or become reticent to discuss them because we're afraid we might refer to them incorrectly.	We should remember to be in a regular practice of sharing our pronouns and making space for candidates to share those as well, whether we experience someone as gender conforming or not; that way it is just a habit and we're not struggling to try to do it at the times we are craving the information that such a practice would provide.

Notice, Name, and Navigate helps you answer the question, *How did we get here and what needs to change?* We know that it is *not* fun to acknowledge these noticings and the associated judgements and wonderings. **Putting words to what we notice helps ensure we don't skip over the effects of our own programming and subsequent preferences for whiteness and masculinity.** And by putting yourself in that place of discomfort, you are working to give that programming less influence over others' lives—and your own.

This practice helps you go upstream to understand how seemingly small, in-the-moment thoughts and behaviors reinforce preferences for whiteness and masculinity.

When you can spot a pattern (Notice), discuss its racist or sexist impacts (Name), and choose a new way (Navigate), you can begin to see the revolution take root in your hiring activities.

REVOLUTIONIZING
HOW
YOU
HIRE

MOVING FROM EQUITY THEORY TO ANTI-RACIST AND GENDER-INCLUSIVE PRACTICE

So, it is clear that US workplaces and the US workforce both need a Hiring Revolution! The question now is, How exactly can we pivot away from racist and sexist patterns, norms, and habits associated with "good" hiring processes, and toward a revolutionary process and consistent practice?

We're glad you've asked! **In part II of *Hiring Revolution*, we get tactical with a deconstruction of what we do when we hire.** It's a true how-to.

- Now that you know how valuable it is to Investigate Your Instincts, we will examine each facet of a hiring process, flagging for you where it's most imperative that you slow down and recalibrate before charging ahead.
- We will utilize the Notice, Name, and Navigate framework to ensure we are addressing identity head on, rather than talking around it, while we hire.
- We will circle back to our Embodied Identity House, stopping in each room and the race doorway, to get clear about all the ways that dominant cultural practices in "traditional" hiring result in predictable inequities for different identity groups.

Team Dynamics has a mixed team embodying a variety of differences that make a difference. **We experience this mix as an asset.** With this range of lived experience, expertise, and vantage points, we are more likely to create patterns, structures, and solutions that will be relevant for our clients, our industry, and our workplaces.

Our mix didn't happen by accident. For you, we have reverse engineered what we do into six parts—and we were careful not to leave out anything you'll need.

Why six? Why not three? Or ten? Because when we broke down our process, we discovered six intentional parts of the hiring process that, ***when approached in revolutionary ways***, will ensure you have what you need to pivot away from preferences for whiteness and masculinity and toward equity.

The parts of the hiring process are NOT in themselves the revolution, but how you approach each can be revolutionary if you pay close attention.

Together, we will resist the *rank ordering* of whole human experiences. We will center equity. And ultimately, we will level the playing field, which has been stacked against People of Color, women, and trans workers for far too long.

The six elements of the process are:

PLAN → BUILD → ORGANIZE → SORT → ENGAGE → DISCERN

CHAPTER 4

PUTTING THE

EQUITY WORK

IN EARLY

Now that you have read part I, you are anchored in the abysmal personal, interpersonal, institutional, and structural ways that People of Color, women, and trans people experience racist and sexist hiring practices. Where has our racialized programming created outcomes in which our favorite candidates all "just happen to be" white people?

Take responsibility for remembering that there is no such thing as only one kind of person (who is, coincidentally, white, male, and in his midforties) that could do this job. If you are preferencing white people or men, it will show in each part of your process.

At work and in hiring, **the processes and practices we've always accepted as "right" often serve to *conceal* preferences for whiteness and masculinity. That's a problem!** Here is a sampling of hiring myths we've learned which have been stated as facts.[1]

- "It's not right, it's inappropriate, it's illegal to consider identity and lived experience when hiring." **Wrong!**
- "It's most important to hire someone who can hit the ground running." **Incorrect!**

---

1   If you'd like more information on grappling with these myths or supporting colleagues in moving away from them, visit www.HiringRevolutionBook.com for a resource that digs into each myth at length.

- "It makes good sense to hire the person with the most experience."
  Don't be so sure!
- "Hiring via committee will make sure our hiring process is not biased."
  Oh, how we wish that were true!
- "Our role is to find, objectively, the best candidate for the job."
  Hiring is one of the most subjective choices you'll ever make.
- "It is the candidate's responsibility to be good at selling themselves."
  Are you really okay with demanding that everyone behave more like white men (assimilate) in order to get your job? We're not okay with that!
- "It is wise and strategic to hire someone who will fit well with our team."
  Is it more important to fit in or stand out? Do you want more of the same?

To evade the myths and dodge the programming and preferences that tilt decision making—yours and your colleagues'—during hiring, you'll need to revisit all of your expectations for the position. Surprise, surprise, that process is most effective when you start with a plan! **When you plan well, you set the solid foundation required to drive an equitable, anti-racist, gender-inclusive hiring process you can feel proud of.** The time and attention you invest at the front end will help you interrupt old patterns steeped in preferences for whiteness and masculinity and set you and your hiring team up for success.

Plan is the longest chapter of part II because the better you plan, the easier the rest of the process becomes. Go slow; take it all in. We are offering countercultural solutions to long-held inequities. Chapter 4 focuses on:

- how you can plan a hiring process that will proactively acknowledge and address dominant patterns of preference for white and male job candidates
- the use of a comprehensive Team Dynamics tool to ensure you are crystal clear about who you are looking for and how you will know if you've found them or not
- completely reimagining your approach to job candidates' prior experience and what that says about whether or not they'd be good at the job you're hiring for now
- who you should and shouldn't include as you consider recruiting help in hiring

ACKNOWLEDGE THE CURRENT *CONTEXT* FOR THIS ROLE

You are never hiring into a vacuum. Even if you are a solo entrepreneur hiring your first teammate, there is no such thing as a clean slate for hiring. Your particular circumstances—gifts, talents, challenges, opportunities—shape your understanding of who you need on your staff in order to reach your goals.

To land the talent you want, you need to know what the role is and how it fits into your current team and company. No, not what it says in that ten-year-old job description you post on Monster every time it becomes open: what the job actually is. You also need to know whether the role you have now is actually the one you want to fill. Would a different division of tasks suit your needs better than a new hire? Are there expectations or qualifications from previous iterations of job postings and descriptions you can throw out? Now is your chance to tune up the balance of your team.

TOOL: DEFINING EACH ROLE

Working from boilerplate or template job descriptions means we're assuming a previous structure meets our current goals. Defining the role each time you hire, revisiting each element—whether it's new or a replacement—means that we don't project our preferences or assumptions about who should or could be in this role. Pushing ourselves to consider and answer these questions helps us slow down, which can help us notice preferences for whiteness and masculinity in each answer. That, in turn, can help us Investigate Your Instincts about each element of the role.

Questions to consider when defining and refining roles you need filled include:

- How many hours per week do you think it takes to complete the tasks required of the person fulfilling this role? Why do you think that? Are you sure?
- Should this be a full- or part-time position? Why?
- This time around, should these tasks and responsibilities be assigned to a permanent or contract worker? Why?
- Based on the responsibilities associated with this role (not what the applicant has been paid in the past), what is the pay band you want to offer? Why? How is this pay band related to other roles? Why?

- What are some of the things that are true about the person who most recently occupied this role or a similar role (think: identities, work styles, history, etc.)? How might knowing who has previously had this role, or roles like it, be influencing who you imagine would like, want, and/or flourish in a role such as this?

Ask yourself these kinds of questions to help bring to the surface who and what you are comparing as you are starting your hiring process. What are the "norms" and/or "ideals" on which you are modeling your job search materials? Do you imagine a white man in his midforties as the best fit for this role because that's been true of everyone who filled the role successfully so far? When you imagine paying to have this work done, are you comparing the value of the completed tasks to the company or the value of the body you imagine completing them? In what ways are you imagining singular or best ways of working—and how is that influencing your search?

Visit www.HiringRevolutionBook.com for a Planning Question worksheet you can use to help clarify exactly what and who you're seeking this time around.

PLANNING TO DISRUPT PREFERENCES FOR WHITENESS + MASCULINITY

Searching, finding, and hiring is *not* a one-size-fits-all endeavor. Remember, equity is better than equality. Evaluate each stage of your typical hiring process with reference to this one role. *Do you need three different rounds of interviews? Why or why not? Will there be a writing test? Why or why not? A presentation? Why or why not?* The answers to those questions depend *entirely* on what you believe you need to know and experience in order to find out which candidates could do *this job*.

Too often, hiring processes seem like a never-ending gauntlet of tests, presentations, and redundant conversations. In our experience, the gauntlet is mostly about whether someone can consistently perform whiteness and masculinity. However, what you and the candidate really want to learn, as efficiently as possible, is whether or not this role, this organization, this company, at this time, is a good match for this candidate or not.

Consider what this job actually requires—day to day, month to month, task to task, and project to project. Check in with people who hold or have recently held similar roles. Find out from employees and supervisors if, based on your current context, the vision for this role needs major revision based on what has happened or is happening throughout your company.

Use that information to plan out a hiring process that mimics this job as best you can. What you ask a job candidate to share and show should have direct relevance to the role for which you are hiring. Cut the extra and include that which is critical to core tasks and responsibilities. Do not plan a series of unrelated application tasks or interview questions. Your hiring process is only as good as the plan that generated it.

Plan to use everyone's time wisely. If you don't, it's both unstrategic and unkind.

TOOL: THINGS PEOPLE OF COLOR, WOMEN, AND TRANS JOB CANDIDATES NEED TO KNOW TO CONTINUE ON IN YOUR HIRING PROCESS

In your planning phase, recognize that part of what you are planning for is how you will successfully lure people away from jobs they already have. Keep in mind that for People of Color, women, and trans people, the likelihood of lower lifetime earnings can mean that leaving a current job can feel precarious, while white male workers might feel that switching jobs poses little to no risk to them or their families.

Thinking like a job candidate, consider how the realities of identity listed below affect what job candidates feel like they need to know, in what kind of detail, and at which point along the hiring process:

Need to Know	→	How do preferences for whiteness and masculinity get coded in these things?
What must I know/be good at in order to be qualified/ considered?	→	Women are more likely than men to follow the exact guideline about who should and shouldn't apply—so it's imperative to be crystal clear.
What does it pay?	→	People of Color are historically underemployed, and women are historically underpaid; transparency in pay decreases the likelihood that you are replicating these trends.

Who else works here? What would my positionality within the organization be? (Who would be my boss, which team would I be on, etc.)	→	If a candidate would be the first, only, or one of a few People of Color, women, and trans people on a team, then knowing who they will be situated near and reporting to helps them imagine what context they would be entering.
How much time should I budget to participate in an interview process?	→	Candidates may currently have more than one job (including a primary job and supplementary side hustle or a caregiving commitment). If you make your process too complicated, you will miss out on time with candidates whose schedules are simply tighter (and/or less flexible) due to caregiving and other job responsibilities. It is a kind of privilege to be able to show up in the middle of multiple workdays for a series of interview activities while trying to keep the job(s) you currently have.
What are schedule and availability expectations?	→	"Regular business hours" is a vague and culturally loaded term (regular according to whom? the tech industry, teachers, legal professionals?). Don't say no on others' behalf, deciding for them whether they could work the hours you are asking. For example, have you assumed that new parents couldn't do this job, or folks in a different time zone, or people who previously worked a night/third shift? Speak plainly: during which hours and in which time zone do we need you available? Candidates can then let you know if that will work for them.

PRIOR EXPERIENCE OBSESSION

Bias alert! Considering both race and gender, there is a predictable likelihood that certain people have not been afforded opportunities to learn, practice, or lead in certain ways. The obsession with prior experience means applicants can get sidelined by the conundrum of needing experience in order to get experience. What does a person really need to do *this one job*?

Formal vs. Informal Work History

Knowing about people's past (such as employment, education, experiences, certifications) can be relevant and helpful in describing what a candidate has done to date. That said, a candidate may have developed all sorts of skills and experiences but not done that work full time or for money—yet.

- What do we think we understand by reading a list of an adult's former jobs?
- What don't we know from reading a list of what has happened in our candidate's life so far?
- What bumps candidates in and out of our yes/maybe/no piles?

Imagine that you grew up working in your parents' corner store. During childhood and adolescence you learned everything from budgeting to cash flow management, inventory, procurement, customer service, and operations related to maintaining building standards and codes. Now imagine pitching your ten-plus years of retail experience to convince a store to hire you as a keyholder right away. How would you expect the store manager to react?

Racism and sexism pervade the work world, which means that if you are always in search of previous experience, you are inadvertently preferencing white people and men. Don't do that. Instead, Notice, Name, and Navigate the truth about what can be taught (and maybe you *prefer* to teach) on the job and what particular experiences someone absolutely has to have before they get to you.

What candidates need to:

Have done before or know already coming into the job (at what level: beginner, intermediate, advanced, expert?) →	*Some examples might include:* • Supervisory experience at the beginner level having supervised 1–3 people at a time • Advanced-level graphic design experience using InDesign • Expert-level sales experience having led whole sales departments of achieving sales goals of $3 million a year or more

Be ready, willing, and able to teach on the job →	*Some examples might include:* • Using Strengths Finder to determine roles and responsibilities on a team • Creating and managing to a budget on an accrual basis • Managing relationships using a Customer Relationship Management (CRM) technology • Public presentations using PowerPoint with only pictures and no words

Now you try it—what would be your answers to both prompts for the role you are hiring next?

Remember this when considering how much and which kinds of prior experience serve as a reasonable prerequisite for employment with you.

ALIGN YOUR ROLE, GOAL, AND SOUL

Given the persistent, pervasive, and insidious nature of preferences for whiteness and masculinity in each and every element of each hiring process, it is not enough to state, "We are committed to disrupting racism and sexism in this next hiring process." You've got to name and claim explicitly what success will entail and feel like throughout the entire process. When you evaluate your process, what will make you say, "We are proud to have stayed true to our values by disrupting those preferences in each and every part of the process"?

Now that you have a clear vision of the role and what a candidate really needs to be able to fill it, imagine that the person you've made an offer to has said yes. What will everyone think and feel about how you Named, Noticed, and Navigated preferences for whiteness and masculinity during the process?

> I will think and feel . . .
> We will think and feel . . .
> Candidates will think and feel . . .

At Team Dynamics, we use a rhyme to help us think about how we'll successfully adapt in order to achieve the outcome we're seeking: Role, Goal, Soul.

ACTIVITY—ROLE, GOAL, SOUL
What is my role? What is my goal? How do I get there without losing my soul?

Role → *To what do I feel responsible? Given my identities and position related to this hire, what do I need to pay attention to? What is expected of me?*

Goal → *What will success feel like in this process? What will have happened or not happened in each part of the hiring process?*

Soul → *What values will guide my thinking and behavior?*

Here is Alfonso's example from when we were searching for our vice president of growth and infrastructure:

Role	Goal	Soul
• I am currently overseeing finance and operations and will be picking the person who will take on these responsibilities. • I am a cisgender man who learned management and leadership from men. • As a Person of Color, it is uncommon for me to be in this sort of role in my industry. • This position will round out our management from four people to five. The four currently are: a gay white woman, a queer Black woman, a straight Puerto Rican woman, and me.	• Remain aware of LGBTQ+ and women being the dominant cultural patterns of our management team. • Openly discuss race and gender and link them to operations with candidates. • Catch my old patterns of leaning toward white women or gay men candidates and ask if those patterns meet the needs of this search.	• Connection—I am grounded in our management team relationships and our company purpose and have the capacity to begin new relationships with new kinds of people. • Possibility—I am hopeful and optimistic and have a deep belief in things being new and transformation being possible.

WHERE ARE YOU AT?! WE'RE LOOKING FOR YOU!

Alfonso: A lot of my friends are fans of the reality competition show *RuPaul's Drag Race*, affectionately texted and tweeted about using the acronym **RPDR**. In the show, drag queens from around the country compete for a winning title and chance to leverage their skills and the show's popularity to launch their drag careers to a broader audience.

Black gender-nonconforming activists have long been on the front lines of major culture change moments throughout history (for example, the Stonewall uprising, which is now considered the spark that ignited the modern LGBTQ+ rights movement). As an homage and a way to help you remember our four-part key to building a hiring process you can feel proud of, we introduce you to our own **RPDR**.

R–Recognize	→	understand your biases, assumptions, and preferences for whiteness and masculinity
P–Post	→	name precisely who you are wanting to find in your job posting
D–Diversity	→	make goals for the mix of your hiring pools and track them throughout
R–Relationships	→	build authentic trust with more communities, be proactive about getting referrals, and work smarter, not harder

We will now unpack each element of RPDR so you can use it in your Hiring Revolution.

R**PDR**
RECOGNIZE

Imagine a role on your team you will likely need to hire for in the next year:

- Who do you imagine will likely fill this role?
  [example: a white woman in her fifties with kids in middle/high school]
- What kinds of people do you imagine *can* do this job?
  [example: men who are physically strong and have lots of stamina]
- Which kinds of bodies have you witnessed in a role like this?
  [example: white Jewish male computer programmer)
- Which kinds of bodies have you never (or rarely) seen in a role like this one?
  [example: I've never seen anyone under forty in this role; I've never seen a Latinx or Black person play a role like this; the last three people in this role were straight and cisgender]
- Who would perform this role really well?
  [example: women]
- Who do you currently imagine doing this role the very best?
  [example: someone who has worked at a corporate competitor for more than a decade]

Key Self-Awareness Questions:

- Who pops into your mind first? Who doesn't?
- Do the people you just imagined match the goals you've stated about a "diverse" workforce?
- Where are your imaginings and stated goals out of alignment?
- How does it feel to Notice and Name who you are imagining first and who you have to work harder to imagine?
- What could you put in place and into practice to close that gap?
- Knowing what you do now, can you identify where the qualities you imagined for the role could keep entire groups of people out of consideration?

RP**P**DR

POST

If you want new kinds of candidates for your job and your company, build job posting materials that describe, in detail, what is involved in this role at this time. Why? Because one of the ways that privilege manifests is knowing some of the insider speak, the jargon, or even someone who has had a role like this before.

Many of the titles we use these days are emerging. New sectors, growing companies, and the evolution of US workplaces means that the jobs available in the workforce are not described as simply as *doctor*, *teacher*, *firefighter* (not that *any* of those jobs are at all simple!). If you do not build out job postings with a granular level of detail, you risk missing out on awesome candidates and accidentally preferencing people who are good at matching their experience to your list, regardless of their actual talent. Are you willing to find the best candidate, or are you relying on candidates' ability and interest in playing matching games?

Use this **Role Inventory** and your earlier investigation into the job's true context to build a detailed set of job posting materials to attract the candidates you are attempting to reach.

Question	Relevance to Race + Gender	Answer
Is this a new or existing role?	What races or genders have we ever assumed or imagined can have this role and be good at it?	
With whom will this person interact each day?	How will this person and their peers/supervisor work across different races and genders?	
How often will they interact with their supervisor and other people higher up than their supervisor?	Given how People of Color, women, and trans people are treated as helpers more than leaders, what will the candidate and company need to be ready for?	
Where do you expect them to be physically? For how long? On what days?	What multiple responsibilities might candidates have given the context of their race, gender, and other identities, including access to wealth to pay for things like child care, transportation, etc.?	
How do you imagine they will spend their time each day? On a computer? On a phone? In meetings? Inside your work building or away from an office?	What assumptions do you make about how "everybody knows" how we spend our work days? Have you projected a white or masculine image onto "everybody"?	
Does this person represent the company externally? When and how?	Will external partners be surprised to experience a woman or trans person or Person of Color? How will you catch yourself managing an employee's physical appearance and communication style to preference whiteness and/or masculinity?	
Does this person manage their own calendar or do others inform or decide how their day is organized?	What level of autonomy and self-determination does this person have? Do they get bossed around?	

DIVERSITY

Are you ready to name the demographic mix of your current team and describe the identities and experiences currently missing from your team?

Are you willing to shift patterns of behavior and truly listen to and change with the new perspective shared by team members who are different from you?

> *Alfonso:* I really want you to stop and take a breath and answer those questions. The answer to both must be YES for the revolution to be successful—and the trick is, you have to mean it.

If you answered yes, then you're allowed to say you want to diversify your candidate pool.

Naming Your Mix—and Its Gaps—Whether or Not You Feel Afraid

Given how whiteness and masculinity are preferred in all aspects of work and leadership, it can be easy to slip into anxious self-talk or storytelling. Racist and sexist hiring practices have conspired to keep us believing the lies that actively hiring and promoting People of Color, women, and trans people means we must want a token "diversity hire" or that we need to lower the bar of excellence to achieve our goals. Your work in setting goals for the mix of candidates includes reflecting on the identities that are over- and underrepresented on your team and describing the perspectives and ideas you are missing (thus undermining your work).

As part of our job postings, we name what we know to be true about who currently works here. Since a potential candidate may not know with certainty someone's race or gender identity based on company bios and headshots, take out that guesswork and self-disclose right up front. Use info you have about your employees; don't guess. We use simple tables like these:

Race	Employees
Black	5
Indigenous	1
Latinx	6
Asian Pacific Islander	0
Middle Eastern/North African	0
White	4

Gender Identity	Employees
Women	7
Gender Nonbinary/Non-Conforming	3
Men	5
Transgender/Two-Spirit/Hijra	2

Some companies inflate their race and gender diversity numbers in an attempt to make themselves and their candidates feel better about their mix. Don't do that. **Tell the truth—whatever that truth is currently.** If you are a large company, consider also sharing the mix of the department the candidate would work in. For example, we encountered one company that included their contract security and maintenance workers when reporting on demographics in order to appear more racially diverse, but that inflated metric was not representative of the day-to-day colleagues office workers would encounter in their work.

Get to know your mix—be honest. Review the data you gathered above, and tour the Embodied Identity House. Now ask yourself, where are the gaps?

What demographic identity groups are **missing** from your current team?	→	Ex: There are no women in management; People of Color primarily fill administrative roles
What do you believe would be the **value-add** if more folks from _____ identity group joined your team? Why?	→	Ex: If more women were in management, we would leverage their perspective as women to inform our strategy. Our client/constituent base is 37 percent People of Color; more People of Color in significant roles could inform our approach.
How will you describe to the candidates the **current identity mix of your team** and how their addition might be new or different?	→	Ex: "This is a director/management role. There are currently two women directors and five directors who are People of Color." This allows candidates to decide for themselves if they are ready and willing to join a team with this mix, especially if they would be the first or only of a particular identity.

It is not tokenizing to set a goal because you want to leverage the best from workers across race and gender—not because it is "politically correct," but because you have a deep understanding that an addition to your team of a different race or gender will improve your work and improve your team. A creative belief that a multitude of experiences would get a candidate ready for this exact job does not lower the bar for excellence. Limited ideas of who is capable reinforce preferences for whiteness and masculinity.

Finding Out Who's in Your Hiring Pool

When you set mix goals and success indicators for your hiring process, you'll need to know who you are and are not successfully reaching in your job outreach. Whether we admit it or not, we are often on the lookout for code in application materials—names, addresses, milestone dates, and so on—that will give us hints about race, gender, age, class, and more. Be careful! Guessing is dangerous. We *do not know* the reality of someone's lived experiences unless and until we ask.

 Do NOT Guess Someone's Race! Your guesses will often be incomplete and inaccurate. You cannot simply look at someone and know what their racial makeup is. You might guess and be right. You also might guess and be wrong.

The same holds true when you are reviewing a job candidate's materials.

Through marriage, adoption, gender transition, whitewashing of names, and more, we cannot just look at people's names and assume an ethnicity or a race correctly. For example, imagine seeing the name *Michelle Hernandez* on an application with the skill "I speak Spanish fluently." Would you be surprised to find out that Michelle is white, has blonde hair, and does not identify as Latinx, but married a Latinx man and chose to use his last name after marriage?

So, how do we find out who we are reaching in our job searches while still operating within the bounds of the law? We're glad you asked! Our answer was an anonymous optional survey. We had Team Dynamics' general counsel, Zaylore Stout, Esq., founder of Zaylore Stout & Associates, weigh in:

> A hot topic question for employment lawyers these days is *"Should all employers collect demographic data on applicants and employees?"* My response has been, and continues to be, you'll secure some great data, but be conscious of the possible legal exposure.
>
> Legal interview questions tend to illuminate an applicant's strengths, weaknesses, experience, and skills, which are then used to determine job fit. Illegal interview questions and practices (ones that focus on the applicant's personal life/characteristics), on the other hand, could make your organization the target of a US Equal Employment Opportunity Commission (EEOC) lawsuit.
>
> Here's some best-practice tips to help you avoid running afoul of the law:
>
> - Participation by the applicant must be voluntary.
> - Enlist a third-party person/entity (who has nothing to do with the hiring/supervisory process) to gather the data in a spreadsheet.
> - Only use the data for tracking/statistical purposes for determining patterns and opportunities for improvement.

In each round of hiring, you'll want to know if any groups or individuals hit a bottleneck in your funnel. Collect anonymous, optional demographic survey data at each phase of your hiring process. Be clear that results are anonymous and not linked to applications; you are asking for responses in order to hold the company accountable to its goals around mix, ensuring a racially and gender-diverse pool of candidates from which to choose. You can review our demographic survey and sample paragraphs at www.HiringRevolutionBook.com.

Based on your current demographic mix and data gathered about your hiring pool, you can build your quantitative rubric for recruitment and track your results. Here's an example scenario:

Problem	there are no women directors in the department currently
Goal	a minimum of 40 percent of women candidates in each round of selection
What Happened	population of phone screens was only 27 percent women/trans candidates
Fix	additional circulation of job postings through women's job network
Do	extend posting period and return to early parts of the process until your candidate pool is consistent with your goals

RPD**R**

RELATIONSHIPS

Entire industries, roles, and job titles are more homogenous than they should be. We recognize seeding the pipeline in certain industries can be a tough and long road. Gone are the days of printing postings and stapling them to community bulletin boards, bus stops, and telephone poles. With so many different digital lists, boards, and tools for getting news of your job posting far and wide, job candidates have to cut through a lot of digital noise. It can be totally overwhelming—not knowing which job to apply for, which company would be a good fit for you, which role you have a good chance of getting.

Historically, your company may have strong relationships with one community or institution and weak connections to others. If you are seeking candidates who have not historically been included in a particular field or institution—for example, women in science and tech, People of Color in architecture—**you must make specific efforts in order to establish and build trusting relationships.** We'll talk more in the next chapter about building out your candidate search and referral framework to better diversify your hiring pool.

Flipping the Script on "Qualifications" + "Required Criteria"

What makes a candidate ready or not ready for this role at your company, given your current work contexts? How will you know? Who will decide? Before you open your search, you must identify the important components of the role. Be very specific. On a daily, weekly, monthly basis, what will this person be doing and need to be good at? What do you hope someone would have done or achieved in their career before working for/with you? Can you name, precisely, what prior experience and practice are required and why they're necessary?

Many hiring professionals and teams are operating from boilerplate descriptions or antiquated lists of qualifications and associated criteria for scoring candidates during a hiring process. As you set aside old conceptions of the role and plan instead for what it is now and what you need it to be, move away from a static or rote set of qualifications. Practice flipping these scripts now so that you can sort candidates with attention toward equity from the very first application.

In the Hiring Revolution we ask:

- Are any of these things necessary, and what weight might we give to them?
- Are they truly as "make or break" as we used to think?
- Are they even the right things to be caring about given the current context of our company and this role?
- Why or why not?

Traditional "qualifications" reinforce preferences for whiteness and masculinity.

Since the advent of the internet, learning has become democratized in new and ever-evolving ways. There are now many ways to gain access to information and opportunities to build and try out new skills. Nonetheless, one commonly agreed upon "minimum qualification" is a college degree.

Across lines of race and class, higher education remains predictably out of reach for some families while accessible (and providing an advantage) for others. **Education requirements in a job posting will, statistically, knock out People of Color and low-income white people, as well as refugees and immigrants, and some folks with disabilities.** If there is the possibility that a candidate could have learned and practiced what you need them to know in a way other than college, **stop preferencing college as the only and/or best way to learn.** How someone acquired their skills matters far less than that they have the skills at all.

There is more than one way to learn most job skills. If you decide that college attendance is a qualification, or a "preferred" qualification, you give preference to white candidates over candidates of color. Cut categories such as "minimum" or "preferred," which serve to rank order candidates before you even meet them.

Unclear criteria also reinforce those preferences. Too often "required" criteria all appear to carry the same weight because they are formatted in a list. Don't fall into that trap! Make your list and then revisit it with the purpose of properly weighting criteria and communicating their relative importance to candidates. **Weighing different skills and experiences will help you focus on criteria that are important, rather than get distracted by criteria that are not a priority given the realities of this role.**

> *Alfonso:* Because my preferences are informed by societal preferences for whiteness and masculinity, I might consciously or unconsciously find myself getting more excited about certain candidates over others. Maybe they share a non-work-related interest I have; they do something I happen to personally find cool. I have to remember that people who feel likable and comfortable to me may not be aligned with my race and gender values and goals for this hiring pool!

To keep your search focused, equitable, and aligned with your goals, practice assigning these weights:

Must Have—deal breakers for this role
Adds Value—given the context of your team and work, you understand this as an unanticipated asset
Interesting—a surprise worth considering, though it doesn't guarantee forward movement
Not Relevant—something fascinating or impressive about this candidate that, given the role, should not determine forward movement

Here's a real-life example:

Must Have—Speak Spanish and English fluently because of our customer base
Adds Value—Has managed a sales portfolio of $2.7M
Interesting—Has a Lean Six Sigma Green Belt certification
Not Relevant—Has a degree in art history

	Challenge with the Current Way	The Revolutionary Approach
Transferrable/ Portable Skills	It is assumed there is ONE best way to have learned something.	Make a list of the kinds of things someone might have learned from various experiences that you believe are transferrable.
Formal Degrees/ Training	What does having a degree tell us? What do we think we know about people without formal degrees or formal training?	**STOP INCLUDING DEGREE REQUIREMENTS. Right now and forever. It is one way, and *not the only way*, to learn and become skilled at something. Instead, include what you assume someone knows or has experience doing.**
Years of Experience	More years are assumed to mean better or more ready—they may or may not. It simply indicates you've been doing it for longer.	Describe what tasks or tools a candidate needs to know, how often they must be ready to use them, and how successful they need to be with them.

Real World, Real Talk: Oftentimes specific or remarkable experiences have allowed a candidate to achieve a capacity or experience outside of the context of a degree or years on the job.

Alfonso: Take me, for example. In 2012, I was hired by a campaign in a deputy fundraising director role. Overnight, I was supervising for the very first time and responsible for raising more money *each month* than I had in the *previous year* at my other job! Prior to that, I had been in program and fundraising roles at a small community foundation.

In 2014, I applied for and was hired for an executive level role at the Minnesota Council on Foundations, a role that, given my degree in public relations and my less than ten years of experience, should have technically been *out of reach* for someone like me. However, the person who hired me was able to consider the totality of my experience, not just my degree and years of experience, and knew that I had what was required for the role. If they would have held fast to a set kind of degree or years of experience, I would *not* have been hired.

TOOL: READINESS + VALUE-ADD ANALYSIS
"This Job Is for You If . . ."

When supporting clients in developing job search criteria, we've noticed companies talking about a mix of distinct things but then messily mashing them into a laundry list of so-called *qualifications*. Upon closer inspection, the areas of inquiry fall into two primary categories: **readiness** for the role, and the candidate's unique **value-add** to the company and context.

Using this framework, we built an analysis to help you **define and refine** precisely what you are seeking and why. It includes an explicit opportunity to Notice, Name, and Navigate the ways that our baked-in preferences for whiteness and masculinity may be influencing who we are imagining could and couldn't do this job. The Readiness + Value-Add Analysis can serve as a powerful tool for reviewing your revolutionized job descriptions.

First, what **traits** do you imagine a person needs to have in order to do this role and do it well? Other words we use in this part of our analysis are *attributes* and *characteristics*. Again, we are working intentionally to think about a behavior that can be shown, not simply personality.

Be wary of one-size-fits-all traits that you want everyone to have. Why is each necessary? Based on the *job responsibilities*, what traits would a compelling candidate need to have: a captivating storyteller, a tenacious problem-solver, fastidious with finance details? Given the role you are hiring for next, based on the job responsibilities, what traits could you illuminate?

Check for a whiteness and masculinity bias after you've brainstormed relevant traits: Does the language or something inferred in the traits you've named accidentally skew our thinking toward one particular kind of body? For example, we read "strong leader" in job descriptions often. Because strength has been associated more regularly with men than women, consider a different adjective/qualifier for the word *leader*.

To be clear, we are *not* suggesting that women, nonbinary people, and trans people are incapable of being strong leaders. What we are surfacing is the reality that such a phrase has been co-opted and reinforced in such a way that a Pavlovian response to "strong leader" would more often than not lead readers to envision a man. We don't have to feel good about such a fact. We do have to deal with the ramifications.

Next, we consider **know-how**. We selected that phrase because it's a better on ramp into someone's knowing than *experience*. Why? Because we have all been taught that only certain experience counts. *What if I'm self-taught? What if I know how to do what you're asking but I've never been paid for it because I made my living a different way?* You get our point. Other words that help us flesh out know-how include *expertise* and *proficiency*. What must this particular job candidate know *before* they can do this job? One way to learn about what candidates know how to do is to ask them to share what they've done (for example, raised $85,000 in three months' time).

Learning about someone's practice sheds light on whether their know-how is at the beginner level and/or very particular to a certain context. For example, someone may have managed staff before. It is different to learn that someone has managed three different teams with more than ten people each successfully toward shared goals. You understand the difference? **Maybe I've managed before, but that doesn't mean I was good at it.** Ask questions detailed enough to find out precisely what each candidate knows how to do.

The know-how section of your inquiry is the perfect investigation into relevant credentials (such as being a registered nurse or an MBTI-II certified facilitator). The key here is *relevant*. If a person's master's degree is in costume design and the role you're hiring for is computer programming, the credentials may be interesting, but they still don't track clearly onto the role.

Check for a whiteness and masculinity bias after you've indicated required know-how for this job: Notice if you are valuing *how* someone developed their know-how over someone else's path. Are you rank ordering their life paths in relationship to one another? Why? How is that helpful? For example, if a job candidate had a specific private college experience, be aware that it is more likely that a white family was able to get or have access to the money required for such an experience. Don't gloss over that knowing. Know-how is know-how. If a candidate can do the job based on their current know-how, move them onto to the next phase in your hiring process.

Last, express curiosity about **uniqueness of perspective**. Remember, this is the readiness and *value-add* analysis. How could this person's perspective add value, given what we are trying to accomplish as a team and whole organization? Other words for perspective include *vantage point* and *insight*. Given who this person is and the life that they've lived up until applying for this job, how have their beliefs, lived experiences, and positionality in their neighborhoods, workplaces, and communities conspired to create their unique perspective? Depending on what you are trying to accomplish, value-add perspectives could include lived experiences such as living as a refugee or asylum seeker, being the parent of daughters, being formerly incarcerated, and so on. The range of lived experiences that could add value given the community you are seeking to impact, the solutions you are working to develop, and the customer base you are working to reach could be vast.

Check for a whiteness and masculinity bias again after you've learned more about your candidate's unique perspective: Do you catch yourself believing that people who didn't attend and/or graduate from a formal program have a fundamentally less valuable set of perspectives on your work and this role? College is pay to play in the United States. Again, resist the urge to rank order perspectives as more or less impressive. Instead, practice setting them next to each other.

When you think about the role you're hiring for, what are your Readiness + Value-Add goals?

- What do you want candidates to have **done already**? Why is that imperative?
- What is the **value-add** they could provide you and your team, given their unique background?
- **Are you seeking more of the same?** Are you recruiting more people like you and/or like somebody else who is already on the team? Why? Why not?
- Are you seeking **particular traits, know-how, and perspective to balance out the team, or to provide a different vantage point** because you think you might be missing something or that there are opportunities to innovate or be more creative if you had more different qualities?

For example, let's begin with something a lot of us are familiar with: the pace at which we work. On our team, we have some people who are wired to work quickly and others who are wired to be slower and super thoughtful. That's good! We're mostly capable of both: thoughtful people can be quick, and quick people can be thoughtful. Depending on exactly what the work is and the precision of the tasks involved, however, naming a balance of traits should give you a hint about what kind of qualities you should be prioritizing.

When we think about **how loaded cultural traits can be**, we think about the difference between boasting/self-promoting and humility. Sometimes a mix of personality and cultural programming gets combined in a problematic set of preferences and/or beliefs. Think, for example, about expectations around introverts and extroverts. Think of the "strong leader" example and how white men are expected to lead meetings; think also about what you would expect white men to not do when playing the role of "strong leader." When we think about kinds of leadership qualities, are we conscious that "highly extroverted people are 25% more likely to land a top job"?[2] Spend some time thinking about why and what are we missing by only wanting extroverts, or believing from an intellectual capacity standpoint that extroverts are the only people who can lead—that's just not true.

---

2   Emma Featherstone, "How Extroverts Are Taking the Top Jobs—And What Introverts Can Do About It," *The Guardian*, February 23, 2018, https://www.theguardian.com/business-to-business/2018/feb/23/how-extroverts-are-taking-the-top-jobs-and-what-introverts-can-do-about-it.

Traits, know-how, and perspective are not simply "good" or "bad"—they are contextual. **What you need on your team depends on the goal of the job and the human beings a candidate will work with, work for, and work alongside.**

For example, if someone really thrives under close supervision, are you able to provide that? Are you willing to give that to someone? Do you prefer to "helicopter" manage because the stakes are high or the tasks are very particular, and you don't want to hire someone who doesn't like to be closely managed? Think this through.

On our team, we talk about humor as a through line of our workplace culture. We also recognize that humor—what is and isn't considered "funny"—is really cultural. In an interview process, we aren't going to ask the question "Are you funny? Do you think of yourself as funny?" Instead, we share, "We work with really intense subject matter, and one of the ways we do that all day is to process and release tension sometimes through humor." That might help some candidates as they think, "You know, that's not the kind of office environment I'm excited to be in," or, "Gosh, I would love that!"

CAREFULLY PLAN THE *ROLE* OF EACH HIRING *HELPER*

Who is qualified to determine whether or not a candidate meets these criteria? You may need particular Hiring Helpers, especially when hiring for a technical role that requires expertise you may not have. In the process, a lot of people can end up getting involved. **Before your hiring team multiplies, Investigate Your Instincts about *why* you have decided each person should help, as well as when and how you need them.**

It can be easy to assume that expanding the evaluation team will disrupt racist and sexist hiring practices, but **more doesn't always mean better**. Clients often tell us about "democratic" or "transparent" processes. Usually this means that a lot of people want to weigh in. The danger here is assuming that if everybody participates, we'll have the most "fair" and just process. Big groups, small groups, and singular people can all reinforce racist and sexist hiring practices.

The involvement of other hiring decision makers and participants should be specific, unique, and goal directed. Be explicit about how you expect each person in each role to support this group of hiring decision makers to practice moving away from preferences for whiteness and masculinity and toward our goals of diversity, equity, and inclusion. (We'll return to the subject of hiring committees in chapter 6.)

EXAMPLE TASKS ASSIGNED TO HIRING HELPERS[3]

Role	What the role entails	Who will do this and why? Reflect on how your choices reinforce or disrupt racism + sexism	At which stage of the process and why?
Track All Tasks	A person who tracks all the tasks, compiles documents, and facilitates committee meeting; also liaises with candidates throughout the process; will train committee on how to track RPDRs (Recognize, Post, Diversity, Relationships) and Readiness + Value-Add Analysis; and will facilitate when the committee needs to reevaluate		
Budget + Boundaries	A person who tracks organizational boundaries related to how much time and money can be spent on the process and holds organizational RPDRs and Readiness + Value-Add Analysis		
Verify Expertise	A person with particular expertise who participates in the second conversation and makes recommendations on who moves to third conversation with the hiring manager and their boss		
Prep Work	Administrative staff from HR and hiring department who disseminate the materials, set up rooms and technology, and order refreshments for committee meeting		
Ultimate Decider	Hiring manager; the person the new hire will report to will say yes or no about decisions at each stage in alignment with departmental RPDRs and Readiness + Value-Add Analysis laid out for this exact hire		

---

3   Adapted from the Management Center's MOCHA framework.

For a blank table, go to www.HiringRevolutionBook.com/Tools.

At the end of the Plan stage:

- You should know exactly what is involved in the role you plan to fill, given your company's current goals and context.
- You have also spent time evaluating who is currently present and who is currently absent.
- You have considered what you will want to be proactive about sharing with your candidates so they are sure to put their hats in the ring or filter themselves out as genuinely not a good fit based on what you're describing.

As you complete your Plan stage, you will also have laid out who, if anyone, you need in order to help you make this hire. Now it's time to build your framework for outreach.

CHAPTER 5

THROWING OUT THE OLD AND

BRINGING IN THE NEW

"Best practices" have, in truth, only ever been "best" for some people. In order to create an anti-racist, equitable hiring process, it's imperative that you level the playing field for your applicants in a number of ways. In this part of the hiring process, you will intentionally build your candidate outreach and evaluation framework—the materials, credentials, samples, and so on that you want them to show you—to attract as broad a pool as possible.

What must you know and learn about a candidate in order to know whether it's a good use of your time and theirs to talk about working together?

This guiding question should drive your announcement and application materials. Don't start from old postings you've made; start from that question. Use the *Readiness + Value-Add Analysis* (see page 96) as your jumping-off point.

As you build your materials, keep in mind that potential job applicants are asking themselves two related questions while they are reading what you've written: (1) Are they seeking people like me? (2) Would they rather find someone else? You need to build materials that help candidates self-sort.

Build is a fun chapter because you get to flex your creative muscles! It's full of real-life examples of documents we built that led us to our dream team members! Chapter 5 focuses on:

- revolutionizing your approach to **job postings and job descriptions**
- reasons and ways to be **explicit and specific**, rather than implicit and vague
- building strategic opportunities for job candidates to **show you** what they can do

RESUMÉS + COVER LETTERS ARE *OVER*

They are. We recognize that this can feel radical, but hear us out. In our experience, **resumés and cover letters have become a contest of fancy formatting and enticing action verbs**. Understandably, job candidates download resumé and cover letter templates from the internet and go about the Herculean task of jamming their whole life experience and professional aspirations into this limiting format. **Comparing resumés and cover letters is no longer a meaningful exercise because these documents have become more similar than different and are replete with opportunities to introduce race, gender, class, and age bias.**

How? If I see where you live, I jump to conclusions about your class background, your political leanings, and more. If I do or don't recognize your prior workplaces, I'm already evaluating whether or not you are smart or important enough to work with us. When I see your graduation dates, I start the backwards math to guess how old you are—and wonder what that means about taking time off to raise kids, how good you may or may not be with technology, and more.

You get the point. It's not good. We can (and should) do better.

What alternatives will help us get to know perfect strangers? Instead of hunting through a five-paragraph cover letter to find what you're trying to learn, take control of the medium: **simply ask the questions you most want answered.** For example:

- Based on our job posting, how do you see yourself adding value to this role and our company?
- Given your professional and personal goals, why are you interested in working for us right now?

Asking everyone one or two consistent questions and comparing answers proactively levels the playing field.

If you really need to see the whole list of everywhere someone has worked, take advantage of online platforms such as LinkedIn. They're not limited by what fits on a piece of paper or muddied up by formatting, so you can access someone's complete work history and professional goals without graphic-design gymnastics.

HIDING THE $ALARY YOU PLAN TO PAY IS BOTH RACIST AND SEXIST.

We know that sharing your intended salary is a hot-button issue for organizations and HR professionals at the moment. We get it. This would be a big pattern change for a lot of people. **Being upfront about money is one of the ways you can show that you are serious about considering candidates across lines of race, class, and gender.**

How often have you seen "salary commensurate with experience"? First of all—the word *commensurate* is *so weird!* Second, proclaiming that illuminates your intent to pay people more or less *for the same work* based on personal factors (number of years on the planet, ability to access fancy degrees or certifications, access to impressive orgs or titles prior to getting to you). Ouch.

Let's dig in to *why* it feels funny, weird, or like a breach of privacy to be open about salary.

Material resistance: We need permission to share salary. It's just not done by other companies in our industry. It wasn't shared back when I applied.

Relational resistance: How would other staff members feel about and relate to this new staff member, knowing how much they get paid? And how much they get paid in relationship to how much the new person gets paid? Come to think of it, how would I feel if my colleagues knew my salary? How might that change all our relationships?

Symbolic resistance: Who will we reach and not reach in our search if folks know right off the bat what the pay scale is? How will sharing salary limit my ability to negotiate upon making the offer? And why does that feel important?

The equity principle of sharing salary up front in a hiring process has given a lot of our clients pause. It can feel impossible, so different, a sticking point in the *revolution* for many hiring pros and institutions. Here is the core of what we don't understand about the logic of withholding salary information: **Are you trying to get away with hiring someone at a lower rate while the job responsibilities remain the same?**

If so, you are reinforcing white-dominant owner control that we outlined at the beginning of this book. This US "norm" actually stems from slavery. You are saying it is okay to bargain on the value of a human and their contributions, and you are admitting you are willing to underpay someone in service to your or your company's wealth building. Double ouch.

If you are not okay with this unintended consequence, cut it out. Decide what the role is worth to the company—its impact, how it fits into the success of your organization—and decide what that role will be paid, no matter which body the person who performs those tasks is in. Then state it clearly: Based on what that role requires, what our budget is, and what the cost of living is in the city/county/country in which we are asking this person to work, here is what we will be paying for this role: _____.

People of Color, women, and trans people are predictably underpaid, and when money is tighter, every little bit counts! In addition to salary details, consider being proactive in your initial postings and offerings by making additional information available very early on in your process or anticipating questions in order to have the answers on hand for interviews. **Candidates' need-to-knows** could include:

- How much, per month, would it cost to make sure that my two kids have dental insurance through my job, and does that include orthodontia coverage?
- What is the difference between the gross salary offered and the monthly take-home pay after tax withholdings, union dues, retirement contribution, and percentage paid for insurance covering dependents?
- Do you have a daycare subsidy?
- Do you support student loan repayment plans?
- Do you cover the costs of renewing necessary licensure or certifications?
- Are your office space and the technology you use ADA (Americans with Disabilities Act) compliant? In what ways? What can be adjusted based on my particular needs? And would you be less likely to hire me because I would "cost" your organization some retrofitting dollars?
- Is your office space easy to get to by methods of public transportation, since I don't have access to a vehicle?

- Does your medical insurance cover fertility treatments, gender confirmation procedures, and trauma recovery services? Is there a deductible, a high cost for seeing specialists, a coverage cap?
- Do you have a transgender health supplement to support one-time and ongoing gender confirmation services?
- What else?

SAMPLE JOB ANNOUNCEMENT—INTENTIONAL ABOUT EQUITY

Team Dynamics has successfully built and retained a mixed team across a variety of differences that make a difference. For the first time ever, we are sharing our "secret sauce" with you. Below are the core components of our job postings. You are welcome to borrow from them. For full examples of job descriptions and announcements, as well as downloadable templates, visit www.HiringRevolutionBook.com/Tools.

As you read:

- Jot down some notes (either in this book or on scratch paper) about what sections, sentences, words, and phrases **catch your attention** and why.
- What appears **new or different** than what you have seen and/or used in a job announcement before?
- What do you think are **some of the implications** of approaching a job announcement this way?

Here is a truncated version of one of our real-life job announcements:

Team Dynamics LLC Job Announcement

Vice President—Growth + Infrastructure

Status / Full Time, Salaried
Reports to / Cofounder and President (Alfonso T. Wenker)
Supervises / Currently 4 staff and contractors, likely more as we grow.
Currently includes—Operations Associate, Bookkeeper (contract),
Storyteller, Digital Engagement and Growth Manager
Key Relationships / CEO, VP—Capacity Building, Director of Client Experience
Salary / $110,000 annually and benefits

WHO WE ARE + WHAT WE DO

Team Dynamics is a People of Color–, woman-, and LGBTQ+-owned
company. We are expert coaches and facilitators focused on helping
leaders and workplaces live up to their potential through intentional and
meaningful culture change. We believe that going to work can and should feel
fundamentally different.

RACIAL EQUITY–CENTERED LEADERSHIP DEVELOPMENT IS THE CENTER OF OUR PRACTICE.

Due to the COVID-19 global pandemic, we are all working from home.
Following a functioning and accessible vaccine, we plan to resume a hybrid
service delivery model: a mix of in-person and digital training, coaching, and
support. Our employees are welcome to work anywhere on the globe where
they can get access to phone and internet and are available for calls and work
time during Central Standard Time (Minnesota).

Read more about our team, our clients, and the services we offer at
www.TeamDynamicsMN.com.

HOW YOU'D FIT IN + STAND OUT

The Team Dynamics' VP—Growth and Infrastructure will play a critical
leadership role in this pivotal time for our company. Our Cofounder and
President has been overseeing much of our day-to-day operations and finance

work; we are ready for an experienced peer to take on leadership of these functions while simultaneously designing enterprise-wide systems to allow both growth and efficiency in alignment with our values.

When we say "Infrastructure," we are including things like operations, finance, information and technology systems, sales and marketing, communications, and project management.

We don't imagine the incoming VP is an expert in all these areas, but rather that they have experience overseeing smart leaders to grow in these areas. In other companies, this role might have a title like COO or Managing Director.

PRIMARY RESPONSIBILITIES + EXPECTATIONS

This VP will manage the day-to-day operations of the company to allow the CEO and the President focus on strategic priorities. This VP will partner as a peer with the VP—Capacity Building and Client Experience Director to create infrastructure solutions to meet company goals.

Growth Strategy + Implementation
- Facilitate a process to create a growth strategy and corresponding infrastructure in alignment with company goals
- Hire relevant staff and vendors to achieve that plan

Finance
- Oversee financial strategy, annual budgeting, and sales projections
- Supervise Bookkeeper
- Prepare reports and projections
- Make meaning of the money—tell the CEO and the President what it means and what choices we should and should not make given the story the money is telling us

Operations
- Oversee and implement HR including handbook updates, insurance selection, and new hire paperwork and systems
- Supervise Operations Associate who will do most day-to-day implementation
- Hire and supervise relevant staff and vendors

Information + Technology

- Assess our current technology solutions in partnership with existing staff and determine what tools, systems, apps, and databases are needed to meet growth goals
- Hire and supervise relevant staff and vendors

Management + Leadership

- Participate as a member of a supervisors/managers group with CEO, President, VP—Capacity Building, Director of Client Experience
- Periodically serve as spokesperson for managers group internally or externally for the company
- Make day-to-day operational decisions for the CEO and the President

This is a "desk job." The VP will spend most days designing and implementing infrastructure solutions and supervising their team. We are seeking someone passionate about playing a critically important leadership role at a fast growing firm.

If you do not currently own a laptop, Team Dynamics will provide a MacBook Pro laptop computer.

THIS JOB IS FOR YOU IF YOU . . .

- Currently feel motivated/compelled by growth
- Enjoy driving multiple projects at one time
- Find joy in problem-solving/pivoting/finding solutions
- Possess strong written and verbal communication skills in English
- Are proficient in Microsoft Office and Google Suite
- Are comfortable communicating using Zoom and Slack

Ready to Lead + Have Skills Needed—We need an experienced peer who has understanding of business growth and operations to join us. You will have supervised people and company-wide projects before. Experience does not mean older, more, or bigger to us—just that when you read the responsibilities above, you have done about 60 percent or more of the things listed.

Personable—Appreciation for communicating by Slack, Zoom, phone, and/or email for most of your workday is ideal (this doesn't mean you have to be an extrovert; it means that you'll be spending a lot of time communicating with many different people each day).

Detail Lover—You like charts, graphs, spreadsheets, and lists, and using them to meet goals brings you joy.

Creative Problem Solver → "Get to Yes" Person—Your job is to find a way to say "Yes, and . . ." to our team, not "We can't."

Relational—To be successful in this role, you will be motivated by and enjoy developing meaningful professional relationships with each member of the team and external partners.

Unflappable—Our current pace of growth may feel highly intense at times; we need a person committed to creative problem-solving, even under pressure.

Diplomatic—You must be able to balance competing priorities and requests without compromising our organizational integrity.

Mindful—An ability to find the interdependencies in each activity and plan accordingly is essential. For example, the CEO assigns a project, your supervisee is out sick, and you need to finish a report to present tomorrow; you have a demo from a new vendor all in the same day. Each is important, and you have the ability to determine what is urgent and what is important that day.

Team Player—Our success is based on what we do together; we need someone who enjoys working with internal and external teams to meet deadlines and achieve goals.

HOURS

Generally available to work thirty-two hours per week, via phone/Zoom/email. We are very flexible for caregivers who might need to provide rides or support, attend appointments, or be available for caregiving. We also need you to be working when engagement is at its peak.

IDENTITY + OUR WORKPLACE

At Team Dynamics, People of Color and white folks, people across spectrums of masculinity and femininity, partner together to advance race/gender equity and build a world we can all be proud of. In this role you would report to Alfonso T. Wenker, Cofounder + President, a Latinx gay man born in 1986.

Black, Indigenous, Asian Pacific Islander, Middle Eastern/North African, women, and LGBTQIA2S (i.e. lesbian, gay, bisexual, transgender, queer, intersex, allied, Two Spirit) people are strongly encouraged to apply. We will not close the search until the candidate pool is 75 percent People of Color.

Our current team race and gender identity demographics are as follows (based on full-time equivalents). Our people may have checked more than one category since their identities fall into multiple categories.

Black	3
Indigenous	1
Latinx	5
Asian Pacific Islander	1
Middle East/North African	0
White	3

Women	7
Nonbinary	2
Trans	1
Men	6

TO APPLY

Fill out this online form. In the form we ask for:

Two to three paragraphs in the email (not attached, write in the body of the email) telling us **why you are interested in this position and how you believe you meet the qualifications.**

- By paragraph we mean a set of three to seven sentences, meaning we expect the length to be no longer than twenty-one sentences.
- You will not receive more or less consideration because of a shorter or longer email.
- DO NOT send us a cover letter. In this process we are seeking someone that pays attention to detail and follows direction. If you send a cover letter, this will be considered not following directions.

Your work/skills/training history as an attachment (as a .doc, .docx or .pdf) **OR link to your LinkedIn profile.**

- We do not have a preference on which one.
- You will not receive special consideration for sending both.
- Our aim is to understand where you have worked before and the types of roles you have had. Maybe you've been an operations manager or a COO before, maybe you've been a nonprofit director, maybe you've been a serial entrepreneur and feel ready to support someone else—we are open and interested in learning from folks across the spectrum of experience and industry.

Qualified applicants will receive a reply within five business days to schedule a conversation.

Position open until filled. Start date flexible—ideally someone will begin full time by October 1.

COMPENSATION + BENEFITS

- $110,000/year, full-time salaried, paid electronically every other Wednesday
- Benefits include health care, dental + vision coverage, thirty days of paid vacation per year, unlimited sick/personal time, cell phone stipend, four-day work week

ACTIVITY—EQUITABLE JOB DESCRIPTION
Reflection Questions

How did it **feel** for you to read all of that?

How do you imagine **different candidates might react differently** to what was included?

What, if anything, makes you **nervous** about approaching a job announcement this way?

What, if anything, **excites you** about approaching a job announcement this way?

As a person responsible for filtering through candidate materials, how do you imagine this kind of job announcement **assisting you and your Hiring Helpers** to run an equitable hiring process?

LET'S REVIEW:

Revolutionized Job Announcements Section by Section

Let's consciously consider the why and how of each section of our job announcement sample.

WHO WE ARE + WHAT WE DO

Name a goal and link it to values. Notice at the end we say "we are expert coaches and facilitators . . . through intentional and meaningful culture change."

HOW YOU'D FIT IN + STAND OUT

Explicitly name how this role goes with your team.

PRIMARY RESPONSIBILITIES + EXPECTATIONS

Short, specific description of the kind of activities this person would do. Notice that some of the bullet points have an example. What does this person need to be able to do?

THIS JOB IS FOR YOU IF YOU . . .

Name some QUALITIES, remembering that value words are highly cultural: be specific about what the values mean to YOU as the person hiring and to your company.

HOURS

Describe precise expectations so folks can decide for themselves whether to apply based on whether this does or doesn't work for them.

IDENTITY + OUR WORKPLACE

What is the mix of your team, and who specifically would you like to encourage to apply? What lengths are you going to in order to ensure the process does not preference whiteness or masculinity?

TO APPLY

Over-the-top clarity of instructions so as not to reinforce assumptions or preferences for whiteness and masculinity. Notice we give examples in the resumé section of what we think the types of transferrable experiences are to indicate that you would not have to have had the exact job before. Plus, when will they receive communication from you?

Be Precise: Don't assume everyone shares cultural norms

Precise instructions help eliminate hidden rubrics. If you're not specific in your listing, you could fall into the trap of preferencing job candidates who have access to whiteness and masculinity.

Alfonso: If I can talk to my dad, who has had a white-collar job, and he can give me tips on what employers want to see and hear, I get a leg up.

Trina: When I lived in California, I was introduced to the burger joint In-N-Out. My friends who had lived there their whole lives taught me that there was a secret menu! It's not posted anywhere—in the restaurant or on the website. I asked, "How do folks find out about this?!" Word of mouth was the answer. To be clear, knowing to order "animal fries" will mean you get to enjoy something delicious. But when you are hiring, don't be like In-N-Out's secret menu! Show everyone what's on *your* hiring menu!

ACTIVITY—COMPENSATION + BENEFITS

People are making a decision about whether this role works for their life and lifestyle. Give them the data they need to make a decision about their own lives. For example: "$60,000 annually, full-time salaried position includes health care, cell phone stipend, flexible work schedule."

Now you try it! Go to www.HiringRevolutionBook.com/Tools, download the template, and practice reimagining and rewriting one of the job descriptions at your organization using the prompts included. Be more specific, stripping away the elements you may have included in past drafts that inadvertently preferred whiteness and masculinity.

LET CANDIDATES SHOW YOU WHAT THEY CAN DO

When mapping out your hiring process in its entirety, create opportunities
for candidates to illustrate their capacity, skills, and unique approaches. You
want to know what they are capable of doing *right now*. **Remember, depending
on who we were raised by, we have really different relationships to telling
others about our prowess.** Rather than assuming a candidate is comfortable
or practiced at bragging about themselves, level the playing field by creating
opportunities for them to show you what they can do—not just talk about it.

What are the actual activities this person will be responsible for in this role?
Rather than requesting a generic writing sample or asking them to solve a
"gotcha!" problem on the spot during an interview, spend some time thinking
about what you need to create a genuine compare-and-contrast between
candidates' skills and approaches.

To get your creative juices flowing, here are some ways you could invite
candidates to show you their skills, know-how, and approach.

Ex. Hiring for a *Website*-Focused Role

"Please send ahead two samples of website pages you have built in the past
twelve months. Also, annotate your approach to layout, length, and design—tell
us a bit about why each page appears the way it does given the goals of the site."

- What we wanted was a sense of the variety and consistency of the digital
  content candidates had each created from scratch.

Ex. Hiring for a *Client/Customer/Public*-Facing Role

"As you prepare for the upcoming Zoom interview with our hiring committee, will
you please consider and be ready to share in five minutes or less two different
ways you imagine approaching the following scenario: a customer calls and
wants their annual subscription refunded, and you don't know why—what could
you do?"

- Different people have developed a variety of techniques for keeping
  customers happy, being curious, and managing conflict. We are curious
  about how folks find ways to engage that are neither begging nor bullying.

Ex. Hiring for a *Finance* Role

"One of our current financial goals is to improve our current cash position. Attached is a sample set of financial statements (not our actuals); based on what you read in this sample, what are three questions you would have for us, and three ideas you would want to pose given our goals?"

- We want to know how adept candidates are at complex financials—in particular, telling the story of what the numbers are telling us.

Ex. Hiring for an *Operations* Role

"We are working to plan our office expansions but are not yet sure how we are going to navigate the hybrid desire of our staff to work from anywhere sometimes and from a shared office other times. What do you think are the key questions to ask that would help us know what the best choices would be for the coming year? Include no more than ten."

- We are seeking leaders who are considering the full range of impacts and influences on the future of US-based workplaces. We're curious, with this inquiry, to learn what is most on candidates' minds as they are in a field (operations) that is transforming as the workforce and technology all transform.

As you wrap up the Build stage of your Hiring Revolution, you will have practiced surfacing and saying that which you may have previously kept hidden. **Recognizing the accidental damage we do by using cookie-cutter job postings, dripping with all the trappings of white and masculine preference, you have now flexed your creative muscles as you imagined a bunch of ways candidates can show you who they are and what they know how to do.** Now that you've built your posting and your outreach materials, it's time to go find your applicants and support them while they assemble their applications.

CHAPTER 6

THE DIFFERENCE BETWEEN
MAGIC AND WORK

Winging it is *not* a good strategy for finding new members for your dream team. A core facet of community organizing is **building a team** to help you achieve your goals. We will share when, why, and how to organize people to help you make a strong hire.

You *cannot* simply post your job announcement all over the internet and expect People of Color, women, and trans folks to flock to your organization. This is especially true if your reputation up until this point has *not* been centered in equity principles that are backed up with consistent anti-racist behavior. If you have had an all- or mostly white board or staff for years, People of Color will pause before applying. If men have filled the majority of your public and/ or leadership roles for some time, women and trans folks will be less likely to respond to your job openings.

Trust building, especially across lines of difference that make a difference, takes time. Imagine being the job candidate really interested in the role for which you are hiring. How high do stakes feel? For you? For your family? For your future? What about if you are a job candidate who is part of a community or identity group that has been consistently underhired, underpaid, and underpromoted?

This chapter is full of tools and tips to expand your personal network of possible job seekers, keeping in mind the layers of how power and identity shape these relationships.

Community organizers are tenacious in their support for creating relationships and networks that catalyze a community to live its values. This chapter shares inside info about how we have consistently found and hired a broad mix of professionals. Chapter 6 focuses on:

- why you should stop recruitment strategies that aren't working and how you can start practices that will be more effective in the long run
- what you can do to build trust across lines of meaningful difference
- carefully considering the mix of who you want to organize onto your team of Hiring Helpers and why

REACH YOUR TARGET APPLICANTS

You know who you are seeking. You've set your mix goals already; refer back to what you recognized in your RPDR evaluation. By this point, and potentially at several points throughout the book, you've thought, "I don't have very many people who are _____ in my network, and neither does anyone in my existing network." That may be close to true, but we would be surprised if you had literally zero eligible People of Color, women, or trans people within one or two degrees of your network. It's likely these relationships are not as strong, authentic, trusting, or consistent as you'd like. If you find yourself stuck due to the lack of racial and gender diversity of your own network, begin here.

Proactively Seek Referrals

Reach out to your people. Ask to be introduced to new people. Ask people you think do great work to forward your job announcement and materials to the people in their networks they think do great work. Actively generating referrals to diversify your candidate pool is the best way we've found to cut through the noise of the never-ending digital job boards.

Deepening your referral network invites you to think and act like a community organizer.

Good organizers thoughtfully create and reach out to a list of strategic contacts. The goal is to learn about shared interests, expand networks, and ask the people on that list to do something in service of that shared interest. Which, in this case, is helping you find someone great for this job! To put this key strategy into action, make and commit to your Referral Plan.

TOOL: REFERRAL PLAN

Name	Meeting Date	Determine Shared Interest	Ask Made	Result	Follow Up
Jeanine	February 1	Shared at a meeting that she mentors trans workers	Asked her to share the job description with five people and share their names with me	Two of them reached out	Thank-you email to Jeanine as well as card sent
Tomás	February 13	Used to run a leadership program for Black and Latinx college-aged men	Asked him to email his past participants	Six of them reached out	Took him to lunch; we've been friends for a long time
Heather	February 21	Was my first boss, doesn't think she knows any candidates but offered to intro me to someone at county EEOC office	Requested an intro email to county EEOC	1:1 with county EEOC, info shared with job seekers' support group	Thank-you note to county EEOC
Yasmin	February 22	We connected after attending a meeting together, and it's clear that her LinkedIn contacts include professionals in my desired populations	Sent a LinkedIn message to schedule a phone call, shared the role, asked for email introductions to four people in particular	Two of the four people followed up with me to ask additional questions about the organization and role	Thank-you note sent

These intentional, personal conversations will likely yield more than an email blast to your contact list saying "Please share this job if you know of anyone open to it." If that generic email generates any responses or applicants, *they may be mostly white people*. We've seen it again and again at Team Dynamics: **when we post on general job boards or send general emails, our proportion of white applicants increases dramatically**. Now, we're not mad about getting white applicants. What we are doing is Noticing, Naming, and Navigating this pattern. We notice and name that white applicants don't currently have trouble finding us. The course we navigate, based on that information, is to determine whether or not our outreach affects our ability to reach our desired applicants, who have the perspectives, skills, and experiences currently missing on our team.

Important: Do NOT blame people for not finding you. Do not assume that People of Color, women, and trans people are not interested or not qualified. It is the responsibility of everyone involved in each hiring process to do whatever work is required to stop giving preference to whiteness and masculinity in work opportunities.

This work may take more time than you'd like. However, you set hiring deadlines. Thus, *you can move them*. If you don't, you will end up making excuses for why your workplace continues to remain mostly homogenous, such as, "We couldn't help that we hired yet another white man; those are the only folks who applied, and we needed to fill the position quickly. *We didn't have time* to start our search over or hold off." In order to end racism and sexism in hiring, you need to *make time* to find who you are seeking.

Expanding Your Network Intentionally

To more consistently reach candidates who are People of Color, women, and trans people, join and become an active participant in more and different communities—both online and in person.

> *Alfonso:* Almost a decade ago, I was running an employment fellowship program for People of Color and was responsible for hiring new classes of fellows each year. I knew I needed to expand my networks to reach more people than I had before. I had just left a fundraising job where I was working primarily with wealthy, middle-aged, mostly white donors.
>
> I came across two groups that were in the process of forming: Minnesota Rising and Make It MSP. Both groups were concerned with issues facing a rising millennial generation in the workforce as well as transforming workplace demographics. I began attending their meetings and eventually joined committees (I was even hired as a facilitator for some of their projects!). **These two networks were completely unfamiliar to me before joining, but through them, I met new people, made new friends, and developed relationships with current and future colleagues.**
>
> Fast-forward to the summer of 2019, when Trina and I were hiring for two new positions. The two people we ultimately hired— both Women of Color—came from these precise networks! I met one of them while facilitating a Make It MSP session, and the other responded to our posting via a group called LOCUS, a People of Color resource network organized by Minnesota Rising.
>
> To be clear, it wasn't simply my *proximity* to these groups that yielded a multiracial candidate pool. **It was the work of building new relationships in new networks over time, by showing up with communities that were initially unfamiliar to me and then learning with and from those networks.** My discomfort in the beginning has yielded years-long connections that are mutually beneficial.

Your Network Inventory

Let's assume you have a values- and goals-based reason to change the race and/or gender mix of your professional network. Let's Notice, Name, and Navigate. Answer the following questions (you can find a printable version at www.HiringRevolutionBook.com/Tools).

Be honest about your current relationships:

- *What is currently true about the race and gender mix of my professional set of relationships?*
- *Are these relationships getting me closer to my candidate pool mix goals?*

How hard does it feel to mix up your network?

- *What stories do I tell myself about POC- and gender-focused professional or community groups? What assumptions do I make?*
- *What body sensations and feelings do I have as I imagine attempting a new relationship with someone with this identity?*

What is my time inventory?

- *How do I currently spend my networking time? What invitations do I accept or decline?*
- *What people, events, and opportunities feel most interesting, comfortable, or familiar to me?*

> *Alfonso:* This isn't magic, and it might not work. Remember my story about joining different networking groups because I had a new job? I'm betting that over the course of your career you have become part of some networks where you are known, you are understood as a trusted colleague, and you have a track record of reliability.
>
> How long did it take you to establish that?
>
> Are the people in that network mostly your same race and/or gender?
>
> Understand that relationship development across lines of meaningful differences is possible AND takes time.

EXPLICIT COMMUNICATION PROTOCOLS CAN BUILD TRUST

Think of how many times you've gotten an email or a text message and thought, *They didn't include an exclamation point or an emoji. They must be mad at me.* Or *They didn't respond for four hours/days; it must mean they don't care or don't like me.*

We're all seeking cultural cues about whether we're liked, trusted, or valued. The same holds true for your communications with job candidates throughout your hiring process.

Imagine what a job candidate needs to know in order to decide whether they can remain in your pool of applicants. Have your communications left them wondering, *We just had this big substantive conversation about the company's strategy and the role, but my biggest questions are from my spouse about insurance. Those answers determine whether or not I can take the job. What will they think of me if I ask insurance questions now?*

How *you* communicate sets the tone for what is and isn't okay to discuss, including:

Frequency of Communication
- Is it okay to call with a quick question?
- Is it okay to talk about benefits and money particulars early?
- Is it okay to send an email with a time stamp after 8:00 p.m.? Will you still think I'm professional?

Modes of Communication
- Is it okay to text with a question since I have your cell phone number from that time you called me?
- Is it okay for me to call in between scheduled calls to get more information and/or to ask clarifying/follow-up questions?

Tone and Tenor of Communication
- Is it okay to call you by your first name—not just your title?
- Is it okay for me to include emojis or GIFs in my messages?
- Is it okay or expected to make small talk about our health and families and plans for upcoming holidays or the weekend?
- Is it okay for me to write an informal or less-formal email now that this is our fifth message to one another?

Length of Communication

- Is it okay to request half an hour of your time to better understand the benefits offered with this role before I say yes to your invitation to move on to the next round?
- What will you think of me if I send a seven-sentence versus seven-paragraph email?

Level of Detail in Communication

- Is it okay to get into the nitty-gritty about who my boss would be?
- Is it okay to ask about the precise take-home salary after tax, benefits, and union dues deductions, since you have the best sense of the withholdings each month?

Expectations about the Candidate's Response Time

- Is it okay (given the reality that I have another job at the moment) for me to take a few days, or over a weekend, to respond to a request from you (especially if it takes thought, focus, and time to compile an answer)?
- Is it okay if I'm not able to call you back the same day you called me?

We're all trying to figure each other out. As job candidates, we don't want to appear too desperate or too clingy, but we're also trying to communicate that we do care.

"AVAILABILITY" HAS RACE AND GENDER IMPLICATIONS

When you have people who are often marginalized in your pool, keep in mind the high likelihood that they are navigating a number of timely and competing priorities. Women are still more likely than men to have the majority of child-care and elder-care responsibilities in their families and extended communities.[1] Women are also more likely than men to have more than one job at a time. And Black Americans are most likely to hold multiple jobs.[2]

---

1   Maggie, Germano, "Women Are Working More Than Ever, But They Still Take On Most Household Responsibilities," *Forbes*, March 27, 2019, https://www.forbes.com/sites/maggiegermano/2019/03/27/women-are-working-more-than-ever-but-they-still-take-on-most-household-responsibilities/#3e8bae1452e9.

2   Bureau of Labor Statistics, U.S Department of Labor, "4.9 percent of workers held more than one job at the same time in 2017," *The Economics Daily*, July 19, 2018 https://www.bls.gov/opub/ted/2018/4-point-9-percent-of-workers-held-more-than-one-job-at-the-same-time-in-2017.htm.

Recognizing these realities, *do not* assume that a "lack of flexibility" in scheduling with your hiring process indicates that they don't care about it as much as your white, male, or more affluent candidates.

DIALOGUES ABOUT TABOO TOPICS

We've raised the taboo of salary talk already. There are more topics that your People of Color, women, and trans candidates especially may need to discuss and navigate with you in order to continue in your hiring process.

Most of our individual circumstances are really, really specific. Real-life decisions about which job offer to pursue or accept often come down to compensation, benefits, our desires for professional development, organizational culture, and colleagues. Be thinking about those things. For example, candidates may be wondering about:

- **Accessibility and accommodations**—Is access to the building that you're working in ADA compliant?
- **Flexibility of work hours**—Will I be able to get my elderly mother to her doctor's appointments?
- **Remote and in-person work expectations**—My spouse is in the military, and we have been asked before to relocate without much notice. Could I be able to keep this job?
- **Full- and part-time expectations**—I am returning to work after needing to be at home to support kids, and I'm not sure yet how my family's needs will all get met once I'm back to work. Will this position really be transitioning to full time eventually?
- **Benefits specifics**—Will your plan cover the brand name of insulin that works for my diabetes, or does your plan require the generic, which does not work for me?

Folks in more financially and physically precarious situations (which are predictable across race) may simply need more details during your hiring process than folks who have been afforded the opportunity to amass a nest egg. If some of your candidates request a bunch of information, ensure that they do not get formally or informally coded as "high maintenance," "unprofessional," or "irritating." Even if they've emailed you four times before the screening call. Instead, create opportunities for private, open dialogue so that each candidate's questions can be answered.

COMMITTEES DO NOT GUARANTEE AN END TO RACISM + SEXISM IN HIRING

At this point, your hiring process may be expanding to include a small group of people selected to help in specific ways. **If multiple people are part of a hiring decision, *everybody needs to be there for a reason*. Their perspective has to *add value* to the hiring.** Explicitly define the role of every individual involved in your hiring process. People conflate "getting buy-in" and "being inclusive" with having a hiring committee or group of people charged with hiring. These are *not* all the same thing, so don't treat them interchangeably.

Don't get us wrong: the days of a single HR person hiring in a vacuum are pretty much over, and we think that's a good thing. But in some ways, the pendulum has swung *way too far* in the opposite direction, and now everyone is involved—the more the merrier! Really?! Why?! How does that make the experience better for the job candidate?!

As you recall from Hiring Helpers in chapter 4, involving more people does NOT mean less racism and sexism in your process. Each of us carries our Embodied Identity House with us to all that we do. The pain, praise, pride, and programming we've experienced all show up when we show up. And as we know, we have each been indoctrinated with messages arguing that whiteness is better than darkness and masculinity is more valuable than femininity. Yuck.

No one operates outside of structural bias, racism, misogyny, and preferences. Period. When you put a group of us together, dominance still dominates. Our racist and sexist programming does not just magically disappear because we're all in a room together. We wish!

COUNTERINTUITIVE CAVEAT: VOTING ≠ INCLUSION

We can have everyone vote on a bad idea and call it democracy. Then we can feel good about ourselves because we can say, "Asking a lot of people means it's inclusive." No, it isn't! **Groups of people can vote on something together and still make a racist or sexist decision because that structure of bias is still pervasive.** Unless you have identified the patterns, individual and group, that prefer whiteness and masculinity, a group of well-intentioned peers, no matter how large, might not make choices that get you closer to your RPDR goals. Don't hide behind a crew of Hiring Helpers by saying, "The final selection wasn't my fault! Everybody voted, and the majority picked the person."

This is downright dangerous.

As you organize other people who need to take part in the hiring process, anchor in the ***purpose of each contributor***.

ACTIVITY—THE HIRING HELPERS "WHY ARE WE ALL HERE?" CHECKLIST

	Your answers	Why? What is the goal of this activity?
Who do you need in this process?		
At what point in the process?		
What are your assumptions about the value-add of their participation? Special knowledge? Unique experience? Particular perspective?		
What better or different result does their involvement create?		
What decisions do they get to make and not make?		
Will there be votes? When? What do they determine?		
How will you communicate to various stakeholders about what was done with their input?		

After completing this checklist (download a blank template at www. HiringRevolutionBook.com/Tools), you should have **a strong sense of the people who really need to be part of your hiring process and the key moments at which you will need them**.

IDENTITIES + HIRING HELPERS

Like your candidates, your colleagues will have questions about why they need to be part of this particular hiring process. We *all* occupy our own Embodied Identity Houses, and you should be mindful of tokenization when organizing your Hiring Helpers as well. Too often, People of Color in particular are asked to participate in all sorts of extra company activities through which leaders want to ensure diversity. Your colleagues have their whole own jobs to do at your company—do you honestly believe they should also be forced to help out with all things related to racial diversity? And without additional compensation, at that? When you request their involvement, they may be wondering, *Are you recruiting me to be on your hiring team because you expect me to scan your application piles for racism and sexism? Aren't you already scanning for preferences for whiteness and masculinity? Or are you asking me to do it by myself? Either way, why?*

White people have to get good at anti-racist hiring. Men have to get good at not just hiring other men. We all have to do the work of interrupting our hiring biases. Responsibility for that work should not be placed on the folks who are already historically underpaid.

Also, please remember that someone who is a Person of Color, a woman, or trans does not necessarily have any training in or history with revolutionary hiring practices. **All of us, no matter our mix of identities, are most familiar with the old ways of hiring—the ones that result in more white people and men in workplaces and in leadership.** There is no secret newsletter that only goes out to People of Color or women on how to magically crack the code to racism and sexism.

Use your whole team. Do not put additional burdens on the same people over and over again, relying on them to be the group's conscience or the sole representative of their identity.

FIRST OR ONLY

Alfonso: I have been the first and/or only in a lot of work situations.

For example, I've been
- the *first* Person of Color at a director level
- the *only* gay staff member on an otherwise all-straight team
- the *first and only* person of my generation—a millennial—in leadership

I have also been very active in many efforts to racially diversify industries, boards, and workplaces.

If you are forming a hiring committee and want me to join it, tell me which Readiness + Value-Add Analysis elements you would like me to infuse into the process. Describe your expectations for my participation and leadership, and which decisions I will and won't be making.

Before you recruit me to join your team of Hiring Helpers, check in about what you think you know about my expertise and experience, given that you know I'm a Person of Color.

For example:
- I am a Latinx person. I identify as Mexican American.
- I have *never* worked at or served on the board of a Latinx-serving organization.
- I have *not* created any programs and marketing efforts with or for Latinx communities.
- I have *not* studied theories or frameworks about Latinx identity outside of my own personal development.
- I am *not* involved in nor do I speak on Latinx experience other than my own.
- If you are seeking someone to contribute broad Latinx perspective, don't invite me to your committee or ask me to be a part of your outreach to Latinx people. My network does not extend as far as your assumptions of what a person named "Alfonso" might have.

Notice the difference? **Are you asking Hiring Helpers to contribute something specifically, or are you unintentionally assuming they have expertise that, in reality, they do not?**

Hiring committees are *not inherently bad*. At the same time, they are *not inherently better* at eliminating racism and sexism in hiring. Hiring Helpers are a tactic in your overall hiring strategy, not a guaranteed solution for achieving your diversity, equity, and inclusion goals. Therefore, use Hiring Helpers wisely, not just as a matter of course.

As you have practiced thinking and acting like a community organizer, we hope you have noticed the added benefits. All too often, people tasked with hiring talk about outreach—which, unlike *organizing*, could mean just about anything—from random internet posts to ad placements that have never once resulted in a hire. During the organize phase of your hiring process, you will make meaningful progress toward expanding your professional network across lines of difference that make a difference. Be overt. Name who you are seeking, and be clear about why. In both your candidate pool and your team of Hiring Helpers, notice when you might end up tokenizing someone if you're not careful. Real organizing requires tenacity and consciousness of a long-range vision as you invest in new and deepened trust and relationships.

CHAPTER 7

WHY RACISM + SEXISM
WILL KEEP POPPING UP

You have planned your process, built your job announcement and posting materials, and organized your networks and strategically recruited relevant Hiring Helpers. Now, it starts to get tricky—in case it wasn't complex enough already! You have reached the stage in hiring when your posting is out in the world, and you're starting to get applications and queries. *Now what?*

It's time to start comparing and contrasting whole, interesting adults.

To sort through candidates equitably, you must come face to face with how your preferences and programming are ever present. No two candidates will be the same. None of them is a fundamentally better or worse person than another. Yet your job now is to continually shrink the size of your candidate pool until you get down to your final choice.

Whoa. Talk about subjective decision making!

As you learned in the first section of this book, People of Color, women, and trans job candidates are *sorted out* of hiring processes with stunning—racist and sexist—regularity.

Research has proven that applicants with "white-sounding" names get more interviews than people with names that are assumed to be attached to a Person of Color. It's a pattern. It's pervasive. It's f*#ked up.

In the sorting phase of the Hiring Revolution—which we must get through in order to start engaging with candidates live during the interview phase—we will zoom in on how to Notice, Name, and Navigate predictable moments of racism and sexism while we sort.

To sort your applications into yes and no piles, you must figure out precisely how you will decide who is moving forward in your process and who isn't. Chapter 7 focuses on:

- how privilege and bias and can trip you up when comparing and contrasting applications
- what it's like to review a work and/or life path that is really different from your own
- making sure you're not diversifying your candidate pool just for show

WHAT TO KEEP CONFIDENTIAL, FROM WHOM + WHY

When you are working on a search and you have done a bunch of work to Investigate Your Instincts, you become more aware of what little nuggets of information **trigger assumptions about whole people**. Sometimes we can't help ourselves, but we can tell ourselves a whole story about what that might mean.

> *Trina and Alfonso:* Using this self-awareness, even though we are hiring pros, we still hide from ourselves information that we know would awaken our programmed preferences for whiteness and masculinity as we sort applications and applicants.
>
> This is nothing to be ashamed of. But if you find that you feel ashamed, we get it.
>
> You can assign a Hiring Helper to organize applicant materials and hide particular types of information so that you can do your most equitable sort. Here are some things we ask our helper to hide.
>
> - names
> - addresses
> - graduation dates
> - fancy colleges
>
> If we do receive this information, we use spreadsheets to track and hide certain info so that it doesn't influence our experience of each candidate. We want to be fresh when we learn about each applicant—unmuddied by everything that society has taught us to be impressed and unimpressed with.

ACTIVITY—CONFIDENTIALITY QUESTIONS

If you really want to consider these candidates on their merits alone, Investigate Your Instincts and ask:

- *What do I need to know in order to decide who we want to interview? Why? Am I sure?*
- *What should I make sure I don't have access to throughout this phase? Why? What do I imagine I will be better at because I can't consider particular info?*

Deciding what to keep in and out of your awareness at this early phase of discernment creates new patterns of what you consider, including the conclusions you jump to before ever meeting a candidate. For your next hire, work with a Hiring Helper to try keeping some info out of your awareness. Notice, for yourself, how sorting changes when done this way.

PROXIMITY BIAS

People of Color, women, and trans folks, low-income people, immigrants, and LGBTQ+ people are all **structurally and institutionally underpaid and underemployed** in the US. It felt important for us to flag, in this sorting section, that when we read experiences that are close to or far away from our own, it can impact our desire to move a candidate further or not. We refer to this as proximity bias.

How do we imagine that happening?

Let's say that from a young age, you began engaging in formal after-school programming and then internships and externships. Those were all pivotal experiences in your growth and development. It's hard to imagine how you would have picked up the skills and perspective you garnered in other ways.

Now, imagine you are reading a candidate's materials and this person's formal work experience started later in life than yours. You find yourself feeling both curious and judgmental. Why wasn't this person working earlier? What did they get to do that they didn't have to work?

Review a different candidate's materials and notice that they worked in the service industry for over a decade. You start to wonder—Did they like waiting tables? Why weren't they trying to do something else earlier? Were they an unmotivated young person?

Whoa—whoa—whoa! You see how fast our brains jump to all sorts of conclusions. **Often, the judgements we make are in direct relationship to our own lived experience.**

Maybe we made some mistakes, and we are judgmental of folks who screwed up like we did.

Maybe we're super proud of our path, and when folks show a very different arc we feel better than them.

Remember, it is nearly impossible to stop these thoughts, feelings, and reactions from arising. Your job is to Notice them when they do, slow down enough to Name what you think is happening, and Navigate your next moves in a way that is aligned with both your goals and your values.

IT'S TIME TO PUT APPLICATIONS IN PILES

Once distracting and bias-inducing information has been removed from applications that have come in, it's time to start sorting. Using the rubric you established in the Plan stage, sort applications into yes and no piles (physically, or more likely in digital folders). **Rather than some intricate scoring system, your initial sort needs a simple yes or no: yes, the application indicates that this person could do this job, or no, the application is evidence that they are not yet ready to do this job.**

We recommend not screwing around with a maybe pile. Why? Well, how likely is it that you are actually going to hire a person from the maybe pile when you have a yes pile? Unlikely. If you are not sure if someone's prior experience is transferrable to this role in the way that you're imagining and want to find out, put them in the yes pile. The yes pile doesn't mean "Yes, you're going to get hired." It means, "Yes, we'd like to schedule time to get to know you better." No harm in that.

As you are working to sort applications with racism and sexism in your awareness, refer often to your newly developed expectations, especially if this is your first deployment of the revolutionary hiring process. Resist the pull of old habits. If it helps, make sure each Hiring Helper (if you are using any for this role) has the rubric printed out or up on screen while reading through applications. Practicing the new way of applicant sorting will require just that—practice!

Remember what you've learned about cultural preferences for whiteness and masculinity in the workplace while you sort, namely:

- The presence or absence of fancy formal training in a person's application does not guarantee one way or another that they should have this job.
- Different cultures communicate about self differently. Some applications may contain glowing self-reviews of previous work and professional ambitions, while others may read as full of humility, including not taking credit for projects and professional wins achieved as a group.
- Because of pervasive institutional and structural racism and sexism, it is highly likely that white people and men will be more likely to have prior experience with managing lots of people, a big budget, and/or a major project. Keep remembering that different bodies have been predictably afforded different access to job opportunities prior to reaching you, your organization, and this current open position.

BE HONEST ABOUT YOUR POOL

When we name that we want to hire more People of Color, women, and trans people to our team, we can do the relational work necessary to increase the diversity of candidates in the pool and still ultimately run a process that works better for men or white people, so as we sort, diversity decreases. Damnit. It's as if we're saying, "We REALLY want you to work here; and we REALLY want you in the candidate pool; *but we're not REALLY going to consider you*." Based on what someone has done before applying to this role, we might sort them right into the no pile, or—just as problematic—put them in the no pile but reserve the right to move them into the yes pile if and when we need to balance out our numbers.

Ouch.

Women, trans folks, and People of Color are familiar with that experience and associated feelings. An organization has bent over backwards to say it is committed to diversifying its staff and leadership. But when they apply, they receive, "We're not moving forward to the interview process because you weren't a good fit at this time." Heavy sigh. Reviewing the job posting again, they know full well that *they have every necessary tool to perform the job with excellence*. It's disheartening. It's infuriating. It's predictable.

We'll say it again: being equitable while you consider candidates has *nothing to do* with lowering the bar. Without question, you need someone who can do this job and do it well. If the applications you receive are not ultimately from a mix of prepared candidates, **you've got two jobs:**

1) Consider whether you need to think differently about how "transferrable skills and experience" are truly relevant.
2) Define what relationship building and outreach you need to do in order to find more and different candidates to be part of your potential pool.

We built a tool called BREAKDOWN to help. If at any point in your sort you discover that an overwhelming majority of the remaining candidates are white and/or male, you can stop and BREAKDOWN—download it at www. HiringRevolutionBook.com/Tools. BREAKDOWN will help you to constructively have a non-judgmental conversation with yourself and/or Hiring Helpers about how your process is inconsistent with your goals; it will aid in staying accountable to the proclamations you've made about your desire for a change in the race and gender mix of your candidates.

Many of us in HR are ready to push back against racist and sexist hiring practices right now. The sort stage is a key part of living out our values. So, with your yes pile in hand, revisit your dialogue and communication goals and prepare to meet your candidates!

CHAPTER 8

HOW TO NOT F@*# UP
THE INTERVIEWS

It's time to get to know your candidates in a variety of live settings. Whether you're meeting by phone, on video, or in person, **the goal is to promote a dialogue—not a performance.**

There is a difference between "giving a good interview" and being good at the tasks and responsibilities associated with this role. Up to this point, the candidates you have been considering have just been pieces of (digital) paper. Live conversations are full of new opportunities for us, as hiring deciders, to deepen self-awareness and learn more about why we feel drawn toward some candidates and away from others. Engaging with the candidates who have made it to this phase could include:

- interviews (1:1 or group),
- sharing/reviewing additional sample materials,
- working through real-life scenarios of this role,
- responding to prompts (either pre-prepared or on the spot) to get a sense of folks' different approaches to relevant challenges of the role,
- and more!

As you get to know each candidate more deeply during this stage, keep conscious about how your racialized and gendered programming influences your thoughts, feelings, and beliefs about different individuals.

The Hiring Revolution invites us to investigate our ideas of what interviewing "should be." We encourage you to start from scratch. What do you need to create a valuable, equitable series of interviews? What don't you need? We give you full permission to ditch the throwaway questions, stop redundant rounds of inquiry, and drop irrelevant interview practices of the past. As you engage with each candidate, ask yourself over and over again, "When and how will I *know enough* to select this person and give them a try?"

Let's get ready to meaningfully engage!

Things can go terribly wrong at the interview phase. Chapter 8 is all about how we can inoculate against the racist and sexist false binaries we've been programmed to believe make us good judges of character. We can and must do better. Chapter 8 focuses on:

- how to increase the quality of your conversations and cut out the pageants
- rethinking what happens in the interview room
- the complexity and care involved in comparing and contrasting whole adults who have lived whole lives

FLOW → WHAT IS AND ISN'T INCLUDED + WHY

What are we trying to learn about these candidates that we *don't yet know*? Our goal during this particularly stressful phase (for job candidates) is to **engage at a level deeper than the cursory questions that got these folks into our yes pile.**

In order to really reroute our brains regarding what does and doesn't need to be included based on what we've already learned, let's think back to questions we've asked and been asked during previous interview processes.

Try your best to recall:
- What kinds of engagement with a hiring team gave you the chance to share the best of what you had to offer?
- Why do you think that line of questioning worked for you?
- In your experience with interviewing, what do you recall being the substantive or breakthrough moments, in which you started to make your decision about who you ultimately did and didn't want to offer the job?
- Be honest: what has felt redundant, or like a waste of time, in your prior interview experiences?

ACTIVITY—WHAT COULD THE FLOW OF ENGAGEMENT ACTIVITIES INCLUDE?

*Depending on the role for which you are hiring, we recommend reviewing the grid below for each hire and carefully considering **how you need to engage** in order to make a hiring decision. (You can download a template grid at www. HiringRevolutionBook.com/Tools).*

Type of Engagement	What are you wanting to understand/ learn?	How long is the engagement and what is the format?	Who conducts/ leads it?	How does what you learn get reported back and influence what happens next?
Phone Screen				
Scenario Review				
Material Review				
1:1 Interview				
Group Interview				
Presentation of Some Sort				

Now ask yourself:

Would you engage in all these ways for each open role you have right now? Why or why not?

Based on the role for which you are hiring, which activities would you want to do, in which order, to funnel down the candidate pool to an eventual list of finalists?

How could you imagine making the engagement phase of the interview process efficient for your job candidates?

How many conversations or interactions do you need to have before making a final choice? One? Three? Five? Why?

We sometimes pretend, in this really litigious society, that we are doing due diligence by seeing a candidate five times, or that it's evidence that an applicant is "for real." In effect, we are projecting the assumption that job candidates are lying or have to prove something to us. Think about things like checking references versus verifying employment. What's the difference? Why does that matter? What are we hoping to learn? In taking seriously our own responsibility as decision makers, we can do better than forcing people through an obstacle course!

As we get thoughtful about what types of engagement we want to include in our process, we must also revisit the kinds of engagement that should definitely NOT be included in our process moving forward.

STOP THE PAGEANTS!

Trina: I have witnessed aspects of hiring processes that feel, to me, like some bizarre cross between a debutante ball, speed dating, and the hazing rituals sometimes involved in pledging a frat. Are you just parading people around? Why? To make an impression? Swing by the office? Have lunch together?

What is your goal when you put a job candidate through a circus? Are you asking people for their first impressions of the meet-cute you just orchestrated? This is a recipe for cultural conformity disaster! All such instances measure is how good someone is at matching dominant cultural cues. Do they "fit in"? Are you "comfortable" around them?

Stop parading people around. Instead, shift to thoughtful, goal-directed engagement. Don't make potential hires submit themselves to random lunches, happy hours, and meet-and-greets and then ask random people to weigh in on your job candidates. This is not a popularity contest or a hazing. Deliberately select individuals or groups for the candidate to meet, and host a discussion about something relevant to the role with a clear set of expectations and a rubric for learning the team's perspective on the value-add.

Each person you ask about a candidate brings their own cultural programming and bias to the interaction. If a job candidate is different in a number of ways from the majority of people in your company, folks might find them more surprising than comfortable. More often than not, folks weighing in about fit are engaged in a subconscious desire to protect comfort and reinforce preferences for whiteness and masculinity.

Don't conflate "getting buy-in" with engagement.

Too often we have watched hiring professionals add more people into the mix, accidentally conflating number of votes with inclusion. Remember: No one operates outside of the structures of bias, racism, misogyny, and preferences. We bring our biases to our group interactions.

> *Alfonso:* I understand that in the past, folks have felt that hiring at organizations was a "behind closed doors" secret. I was raised Catholic, so I imagine it like the white smoke coming out of the Vatican when cardinals choose a pope!
>
> The goal of mindful engagement with job candidates is NOT to create or keep secrets. We need something different. But the antidote is NOT to bring more colleagues in with things like:
>
> - "Hey, we're going to stop by your cubicle in a few minutes" or
> - "We'd love for you to drop by the interviews and weigh in" or
> - "We've asked a final candidate to join our virtual lunch and learn and do a Q&A" with the secret expectation that candidates will be casually impressing people and making them laugh while looking cute and eating (without getting anything on their shirt), and also asking good questions, being collegial, etc., in that format.
>
> I have been part of these interactions—I'm sweating just thinking about them!

If you're expecting candidates to engage with more staff people in your process, be certain you have a precise reason for *why*. For example: There might be a real reason why you want Todd to meet Jennifer or Jerome to connect with Elliot. *Have* a reason.

If someone has final approval or veto power on this hire, what kind of interaction do they need to have with your job candidate in order to give the sign-off required?

Is contact necessary at all? Or is it about reviewing relevant materials, receiving analysis from your team of Hiring Helpers, and talking through your compare-and-contrast of qualified candidates?

For many workplaces, the COVID-19 global pandemic created new opportunities to operate creatively while we couldn't safely interview folks in person. How has that shifted your interview expectations moving forward?

- What about interviewing remotely do you imagine felt easier for the job candidate compared to in-person interviewing? And easier for the Hiring Helpers?
- What about interviewing remotely do you think felt harder for the job candidate? And Hiring Helpers?

Rather than just going back to what we used to do, what are you taking from that experience? How do you want to be mindful about which format to use when you hire now and into the future? Did some people like interviewing online more? Who liked it less?

Equity!!! There is no one-size-fits-all option that works best for everyone. Can you imagine a world where different candidates engage in different ways and you are clear about how that does not advantage or disadvantage a particular candidate?

Identical is not the goal. You may not need to ask every candidate every single question on your list: based on their application materials, you might know some answers already. And you may not need to see everyone on camera if one of your candidates doesn't have a access to a webcam. You can still compare and contrast candidates, mindful of your preferences along the way.

INTERVIEW QUESTIONS → A PAST, PRESENT, AND FUTURE ORIENTATION

So you've taken some time to consider which engagement activities from your past have felt meaningful and which have not. As you begin to craft your questions for candidates who want to fill this role, consider structuring inquiries around the past, present, and future. For example:

ACTIVITY—PAST/PRESENT/FUTURE

[Past] Tell us a story about a time when you _____.

had to reach a goal following a major budget shortfall.
used evaluation to pivot strategy.
successfully managed a team toward a shared goal.
What else?

[Present] Tell us about how you would approach _____.

determining order of operations given our newest priorities?
defining and refining relevant success indicators?
balancing our current competing priorities, rebuilding after the hits we took
during COVID-19 and the subsequent economic fallout, staying on top of relevant
technological advances? What else?

[Future] As we consider our future as a company, _____.

how do you imagine you could uniquely contribute to our growth?
what challenges do you think we should be preparing for now?
how would you go about preparing? How do you imagine expanding
our reach, impact, and/or sales? What else?

Way too often, we see interview questions that are grounded almost entirely in the past. That results in an obsession with prior experience, which does not give your candidate room to share how they would imagine applying everything they have learned and done up to today.

If interviews become a contest of who has a more impressive past, white people and men will win.

Consider reviewing the questions submitted by you and your Hiring Helpers to balance out past, present, and future orientation and truly get a sense of what differentiates your candidates, beyond what they've done prior to finding you. (You can download our list of interview prompts spanning the past/present/future orientation at www.HiringRevolutionBook.com/Tools.) **We also recommend using your *Readiness + Value-Add Analysis* to create relevant, strategic, and meaningful interview questions.**

Imagine you're hiring for a sales job that involves sending someone to a lot of events to grow your list of potential customers. This is how you might use the analysis and the candidate's application materials to generate questions for the interview:

	Requirement	Interview Question
Traits	Can attend events with dozens of strangers and successfully meet five to ten people and leave with their contact information.	We expect our sales team to attend events. Usually these events are filled with potential customers who are at a peer level with our sales people. They are mostly white and male. Talk to us about how you would navigate the events and leave with the contact information of five to ten people.
Know-How	Has sold a product to a list of cold prospects before.	I see on your resumé you've sold to cold contact lists—great, that's what we're seeking. Do you have a way you like to do that? Are there questions you have about our expectations for how that happens?
Perspective	Has NOT worked in our industry and can bring sales ideas from other industries to help us innovate.	What are the sales tips and tricks you learned from your previous industry? Which of those do you want to try in ours, of course not knowing if we've tried them or not?

ASK FOR RELEVANT MATERIALS + PRESENT RELEVANT SCENARIOS

Beyond the initial application materials you requested, now is the time to **move from the broad to the specific** in your hiring process. In reality, what is the context of your company, and what are you seeking in the next person to fill this role? What is it that you need the person in this job to be really good at? Your goal is to create conditions in which candidates can show you the uniqueness and strength of their value-add.

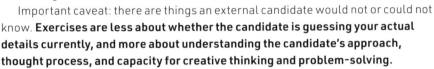

Important caveat: there are things an external candidate would not or could not know. **Exercises are less about whether the candidate is guessing your actual details currently, and more about understanding the candidate's approach, thought process, and capacity for creative thinking and problem-solving.**

In your revolutionary interviews, don't pick scenarios that happen to be most interesting to you. Instead, focus on scenarios that feel genuinely relevant to this precise role.

For example:

- Would the person in this staff role often be the first person to write something—so you'd like a prompt for some **writing from scratch**? If yes, be sure to give clear parameters, such as 500 words and/or a presentation or paragraph format, and a realistic completion period. (For example—if this is something a person in the job could write, revise, and mull over for a few hours or overnight, the scenario shouldn't demand a ten-minute turnaround.)
- Would the person in this role have **final approval** on certain materials seen by the public? If yes, you could give each candidate an example and ask them to identify mistakes in it.
- Do the responsibilities of this role include **managing** more than five staff people? Create a scenario and give candidates an opportunity to talk through how they would support a supervisee who was not reaching their goals.
- Would the person in this job be responsible for **navigating the complexities of a budget** that may need to get cut or changed mid-fiscal year? If yes, could you give a scenario that doesn't have singular "right" answers, but instead creates the opportunity to get a sense of how different candidates approach making necessary changes?

Lastly, if scenarios and/or additional materials will be helpful, be sure not to create gotcha moments—that is, trick questions or scenarios where lots of insider knowledge would be needed to give satisfactory answers. These are not ultimately helpful.

Judge substance: don't let yourself get wowed by things like formatting if the job is not, in fact, a design job. Remember, white people and men have been given the leg up on how to perform in "impressive" ways during interviews. Keep revisiting your goals and stay focused on the different value ads proposed by each candidate.

If you want to see additional materials, consider how much time the person in this role would have to build something and give candidates that time. If some candidates are able to create "prettier" materials because they have financial access to better tools, keep that in mind as you acknowledge the likelihood that white folks and men typically have more access to fancier tech, given the reality of pay disparities by identity.

ROLES DURING THE ENGAGEMENT PHASE

Recall the earlier conversation about hiring by committee? It is imperative that everyone be clear about their participation during the engagement phase of hiring. Just because a bunch of people are involved doesn't mean they all have equal say in the final choice. Every Hiring Helper must be involved for a reason and have a clear goal or task.

It's important to set realistic expectations for strategic engagement. Not all Hiring Helpers will be involved in the process from beginning to end. Not all Hiring Helpers will meet or interact with the candidate. Why? Because some serve as strategic contributors to the process, offering their expert opinion, recommendation, and/or unique vantage point.

Be clear about the decision-making criteria and decider at each phase of the hiring process. Be clear about who is engaging with the application materials, the applicant, and the final decision.

Upon final selection of your new colleague, take time to appreciate all the folks who helped. Report back, sharing how their thinking contributed to your final choice and how their particular perspectives added value to the hiring process in particular and overall.

USE PROTOCOLS TO MANAGE HOW RACE AND GENDER INFLUENCE YOUR CONVERSATIONS ABOUT CANDIDATES

You're in the engagement phase of hiring, so your pool gets smaller as you go along. In order to keep people in or remove them from your pool, you talk to yourself and other people about what makes you prefer one candidate over another.

These seemingly casual conversations in the in-between moments of a hiring practice can inadvertently do the most damage because our preferences for whiteness and masculinity lurk just under the surface. Unless we make a plan to mitigate them and re-pattern the way we discuss candidates, we risk falling into the old traps of baked-in preferences for whiteness and masculinity. You can't be too careful in this regard.

Because no one operates outside of the structures of bias, racism, misogyny, and preferences, **we can use protocols to help keep our actions aligned with our values**. What are protocols? They are actions we take on an if/then pattern: If this _____/then _____. It's a way to plan ahead and prepare for actions we will need to take when likely things happen. Protocols can be used for big and little moments. For example:

> If a client calls Trina "Katrina," then Alfonso gives a quick out-loud reminder that her name is Trina.
>
> If a client uses the word Hispanic to refer to Alfonso, then Trina gives a quick out-loud reminder that Alfonso does not use that word—it's not accurate when referring to him or his family's migration experience. You can use either Latinx or Mexican American.

You might read these examples and ask why we don't just "stand up for ourselves"—and of course we do! But one of the ways we spread discomfort around on a mixed team is to not force folks to take a defensive stance about themselves all the time. We've decided on these short and sweet acts of solidarity as our preferred protocols if these particular mistakes happen and we're both in the room to correct them.

With those protocols in mind, here is one example of how we might discuss, develop, and use protocols to help us Notice, Name, and Navigate when our preferences for whiteness and masculinity rear their ugly heads when we compare and contrast job candidates.

Phase	Who	Goal	Protocol for what is reported or discussed
Application	HR reviews	-Meets Readiness + Value-Add Analysis aligned with RPDR goals	*Okay* → describe as objectively as possible what application elements stood out more than those that didn't move forward *Not Okay* → talking about an application being stronger because of its formatting, response length, or feeling "relatable" unrelated to the analysis
Phone Screen	HR + Hiring Manager	- Understand shared interest between company and candidate - Narrow to a group of people you would be excited to add to the team in alignment with RPDR goals and Readiness + Value-Add Analysis you need/want to add	*Okay* → discuss examples they used and how that meets your goals *Not Okay* → giving preference to people who are more expressive emotionally as a way to tell they are more excited—excitement looks different on different people
Live Zoom Face-to-Face	Peers + Hiring Manager	- Experience candidate interacting with the actual daily activities - Candidate understands your expectations	*Okay* → discussing how their presence would add value *Not Okay* → discussing their appearance or if you could imagine being their friend
Decide	Hiring Manager	-Decide between people that could do the job	*Okay* → describing to the team how their specific value-add meets your RPDR *Not Okay* → talking about how everyone is going to "like" them

ACTIVITY—PROTOCOLS

Question for you: For the stages and roles you lay out, what is okay and not okay at each stage? Why?

PREFERENCES, PROGRAMMING + PROJECTING OUR OWN CULTURAL CUES

The engagement phase of hiring is when human beings really jump off the page and become real, whole people! **This presents an additional opportunity to Notice, Name, and Navigate how you make meaning of job candidates' behaviors—especially those that might be really different than your own.** Body language, tone of voice and way of speaking, how we show we care about something, what we laugh at—all these things have been influenced by who we were raised by, what kinds of people we've been around, and what we've been praised or punished for.

Here are some examples of cues that could mean ANYTHING:

Gaze	*Maintaining direct eye contact vs. moving eyes or eyes not looking at interviewer*
Steadiness of Voice	*Experience a tremble vs. no tremble*
Hand Motions	*Still hands vs. wringing of hands or gesturing*
Posture	*Sitting still vs. adjusting neck, back throughout*

It is valuable for each of us to do the work to remember that our individual behavior is not universal and/or the only good way to exhibit being professional, prepared, passionate, or confident. We practice noticing reactivity in our body, heart, and head when somebody does something that is *out of pattern* culturally for us. We practice a pattern of self-inquiry when a candidate behaves differently than we ourselves might. Questions helpful in disentangling our early imprinting and programmed preference for whiteness and masculinity include: *What have we decided these different behaviors mean? Indicate? Prove? Which behaviors turn us off? Make us nervous or unsettled? Why do we think that is? Which behaviors do we find ourselves wishing candidates would emulate?*

For example, how would you react if a job candidate, at the start of an in-person interview, greeted you with a bow? What about kissing you on your right cheek? What about a greeting that starts as handshake and then turns into a half hug where they pull you in a little bit for a back pat? Now, how might your reaction to each of these different cultural norms for professional greetings change based on your gender and race and the gender and race of the candidate?

The truth is, there are *all* sorts of cultural cues that signal "Hello, happy to see you, excited to connect." Notice for yourself which of the above scenarios sounded lovely and which would be jarring if you were to experience them in an interview setting.

Difference, for some of us, can result as dissonance in our bodies.

If you find yourself thinking a version of, "We're in the US, people should know that the appropriate thing to do is a brief handshake with some eye contact," reflect and remember that you are asking folks from different cultural communities to assimilate to your way of being.

Now consider this example: what if a job candidate is nursing a baby during a Zoom interview? Stick with us. *Can you imagine a scenario where you gave candidates just a few windows in which to schedule, and the available time slot for this candidate happened to overlap with the baby's feeding time? Could you live through that? Could you concentrate? Do you believe that it is inappropriate for a parent to feed their child?* We share this example to remind you that even things that may, at this moment, sound just too far out of cultural pattern for you could in fact be possible without any negative consequences.

Our identities and subsequent experiences influence how we experience job candidates during the engagement phase of the hiring process in all sorts of ways. Based on how we ourselves do and don't behave, we read into other people's behavior—big time!

Emotional Intelligence Alert

Beware of the commonplace conversations in work settings about EQ or "emotional intelligence." We have heard casual discussion about job candidates' perceived EQ between interviews. *Be alert!* When we talk about whether or not we think candidates could "pick up on cues," or that they seem to "really understand the energy of our team," what we actually might be judging is how well they are able to *behave like us, behave like white workers, and/ or behave like strong men.*

WHAT CAN HAPPEN WHEN WE BEGIN DISCUSSING
HOW CANDIDATES MAKE US FEEL

We can think to ourselves, or even say out loud to our colleagues, that an interview just "didn't feel good" to us. We can't put our finger on why, but "he just didn't feel friendly." Practice parsing out the truth of the behavior you're evaluating. Just like the last candidate, he came in, he sat down, he took notes, he asked questions, he left. What happened during those very regular activities that I did not love, didn't like, didn't warm to, or just didn't feel good about?

As adults, many of us behave the way we do because we think it is the best or ideal way to behave. We may have tried other ways and decided this kind of behavior aligns best with our integrity or feels most authentic to us. So it can feel confusing when other people aren't behaving the same way we are.

Questions for you to consider:

- How are you *projecting* your ideas of nervousness, comfort, preparedness, professionalism, and more throughout a recruitment and interview process?
- What could be the *accidental impacts* of asking fellow Hiring Helpers, "So what did everybody think about the candidates?" or "Who was your favorite from that round?"

Throughout the engagement stage of hiring, you may have interacted in a number of ways with the candidates in your yes pile—in email, over the phone, via video chat, or through in-person interview time. You have engaged with their application materials and maybe even with the answers they have provided as part of pre-work or scenario responses you asked them to complete. You are building and deepening real relationships with real people. In order to move from the engagement phase to discernment, it is your job to make sure you engaged in all the ways you needed to in order to have the information you need.

Moving away from arbitrary or overly generic interview questions and formats will likely have been a relief. You may now feel as though you really know what these candidates are capable of and seeking. As you prepare to move on to selection, Notice and Name the mix of your remaining pool and Navigate what you want to do, given that reality and your diversification goals. *You* set the timeline for this hire: it is *your* company. So, if at any point you need to add or shift something about engagement to create a level playing field, *you* make that call. Once you've engaged enough, it's time to pick your person.

CHAPTER 9

COMPARING AND CONTRASTING

RATHER THAN RANK ORDERING

All of your hard work (and that of your Hiring Helpers, if you have some) in comparing and contrasting whole adults is about to pay off! It's time to go from your pool of finalists to actually making the offer. Last check: did you hold yourselves accountable to the finalist pool you claimed you wanted? What kinds of people did and didn't advance to the finalist pool? You might use the BREAKDOWN tool again here. (Visit www.HiringRevolutionBook.com/Tools.)

We're picking who we want to work with. Who we want to be near during a lot of hours of our waking life. Who we want to work on hard projects with. Who we want to do mission-driven work with. Who we want to grow professionally alongside. It's a really personal decision. Don't kid yourself that it's not.

We want to tell ourselves that we're being fair and objective. Again, hiring is really *subjective*. You will still need to make judgments, but with all these tools in your toolbox, you can align your decision with your values and your goals.

The process is almost complete; don't fall back on old habits now! Continue the momentum to make this and future hiring decisions more equitable. Chapter 8 focuses on:

- moving beyond simple comparisons of prior experience to more holistic consideration
- how common discussions about "fit" and "hit the ground running" have racist and sexist implications

ALL CANDIDATES ARE QUALIFIED—WHO DO WE PICK?

How do you equitably decide who to hire? Be clear about the point in the hiring process at which you want conversations about qualifications to be over. What do we mean? And why is this important?

You always reach a point in the process where all the remaining candidates *could*, theoretically, do this job. For us, that's our finalist pool. By the time we are down to three or four people, we're clear that each person is capable of the tasks required. Would they each do it differently? No question—they are different people. But all of them could do the job and do it well: they have what it takes.

Now your discernment needs to shift. Don't hide behind "whoever is the *most qualified* deserves this job." They are all qualified. Period. If the win always goes to the *most qualified* candidate, white people and/or men will win the race over and over again.

Getting to your final selection invites you to extend your framework past that race. A better frame at this stage is, ***Given our current context, from among this pool of capable adults, who adds the value we need for our org, and our team, right now?*** To better understand this framing, ask yourself these questions:

- Consider one or more of your current job openings. Given your current context, what value-adds from the Readiness + Value-Add Analysis do you imagine would be the difference in selecting one candidate over all others?
- What value-add feels most important, given that your context might be different from role to role and from time to time at your company?

DISCUSS *DISTINCTIONS* RATHER THAN RANK ORDER

It takes practice to consider folks in this different way, but we want to get out of this Likert scale rank ordering and instead do a meaningful compare-and-contrast. Set aside the scale from better to worse. Instead, acknowledge difference.

- It might be that somebody worked in higher ed, and somebody worked in corporate.
- Somebody has worked internationally; somebody has worked domestically.
- Somebody has a certificate, and somebody learned on the job.

Okay. Those are just differences. How do we feel about those differences? And what do those differences in lived experience and perspective mean to us as we're considering who to select?

Go back to your rubric. Stay anchored in your goals.

No matter how much we wish for it, there is no crystal ball at this phase to guarantee you will like working with this person and they will like working with you. Once you're comparing and contrasting capable adults, you can get stuck in a round of "Oh my gosh, both of these folks are so good" or "All four of these people are incredible—how am I going to choose between them?" We've been there! Go back to some of your initial considerations:

- Who are we seeking and why?
- Based on what our organization is up against, now and in the future, what kinds of teammates would help us be successful?
- What do we have enough of already? (for example, particular traits, experience, relationships)
- What would we benefit from having more of?
- What might this person have/know/be able to do that could make us all better?

Caveat: Don't let weird rubrics or things you've learned along the way, formally or informally, create justifications for hiring or not hiring someone for reasons that are not relevant given your goals. *Don't* tell yourself, "I've learned through talking with her that she has four kids, so I bet she'd be distracted." Don't you dare do that! That is not a reason for a yes or no between qualified adults. *Don't* tell yourself, "I'm going to hire this person over that person because they live closer." Why is that important if you have been clear about expectations for onsite time? If each candidate has said they are willing to meet those expectations, it's not your business where people go to sleep. You get the point!

Catch How Race and Gender Have Factored into Our Final Impressions

We were working with a client that held a cocktail party as part of their hiring process and asked attendees to fill out little slips of paper giving their thoughts on each one of the final candidates. When the participant feedback was cross-referenced with identity, **there was a clear preference for how white people handled themselves at this cocktail party.**

In this case, Women of Color who were Asian Pacific Islander handled themselves differently than the white finalists. The feedback referred to the two female API finalists with words like "shy," "reserved," "not as friendly," and "I didn't get as good of a sense of their personality."

When we think culturally about who has been taught to behave in what ways, imagine: *What if I've been taught to listen before I speak, especially to elders? What if I've been taught that if I am a guest and not the host, I should not speak first or ask a ton of questions? What if I was taught that professionalism and intellectual rigor are indicated by how deeply I listen?*

Breathe for a second. Are any of those questions triggering for you? Take time now to reconnect to your belief that white ways of being are not the only valuable ways to behave on the planet.

Breathe one more time. Connect to your belief that People of Color, women and trans folks are, of course, capable of being fantastic leaders. There is more than one way to lead.

"FIT" + SELECTION

If your goal is to transform the workforce and the economy toward racial and gender equity, the candidates you meet and choose and the process you participate in **won't "fit" or feel like what you've done before**. The experience will be loaded with discomfort. You are upending the status quo. You are connecting to the truth that this role could be performed well in several different ways, by several different people, and not just in one white and male way.

If we've determined in our RPDR that we would like to increase the number of senior managers of color, and we are clear that there are not currently any senior managers of color, it's likely we will experience candidates of color as not quite a "good fit." Be aware of when you find yourself feeling trepidatious about a candidate "gelling" with the team given their "communication style." You catch the racism and sexism there?

- Why on earth is fitting in more important than **standing out**?
- How are we **willing to be changed** with the new addition of this whole human?

Maybe a candidate's communication style is different. Maybe they come from a different background or have a different expertise than you've worked with before. Maybe they're switching sectors and use a different shorthand than you. They won't feel like the other people who came before them. Ask yourself: is it our baked-in preferences for whiteness and masculinity saying that a person does or doesn't make us feel good?

Centering comfort in the form of "fit" means racism and sexism will win out in hiring every time.

REFERENCE CHECKS + BACKGROUND CHECKS ARE RACIST

Reference and background checks continue to show up in a lot of our clients' hiring processes. We have real concerns. Unless you are crystal clear how these will add value to your process, and not in fact reinforce cultures of surveillance that disproportionality target and penalize People of Color and trans folks, this phase can erode trust, reinforce bias, and give power to people who are not the job candidate to influence your final decision.

References Differ

Our clients who are hiring professionals tell us with regularity that reference checks are not adding value to their hiring process. In fact, most folks find it a waste of time. It's a formality, a habit, that does not result in a decision different than the one made prior to the reference check.

Additionally, from a race and class perspective, reference checks can skew your perception of a candidate if and when someone has access to a reference with a fancy title or reputation. If some folks only have a family member or friend to vouch for them, would you take their candidacy less seriously? Perhaps.

Former Felony Convictions

We feel so passionately about former felony convictions and employment that we dedicated one of our entire *BEHAVE* podcast episodes to how the over-policing of communities of color in the US has made it harder for People of Color to get jobs, get promotions, and build wealth and health.

Because of a racist justice system, prerequisites of not having former felony convictions automatically preference white job candidates.

> *Trina:* Throughout my career, I have had incredibly smart, talented, impactful people work for me that happen to also have former felony convictions. If I had put this arbitrary barrier in place, I would have never gotten to work with these colleagues. That would have been a loss for me as well as the organizations we served together.

For very particular roles, such as working with minors or driving a moving vehicle for a living, it may make sense to check convictions. However, the information you get if and when you conduct background checks can lead to multiple decisions on your part. The gist of it is this: in the United States currently,

- People of Color are overly policed, overly charged, and overly convicted.[1]
- Transgender, nonbinary, and gender-nonconforming people (especially those of color) are overly policed, overly charged, and overly convicted.[2]
- Felony convictions are not a viable litmus test for discerning the "good" from the "bad" people.

Break the cycle of people not being able to get back on their feet by allowing adults the chance to get back to work! For our full discussion, download the episode and listen (or read the transcript) for free at www.TeamDynamicsMN.com/Season-1.

---

1   Robin Smyton, "How Racial Segregation and Policing Intersect in America," *TuftsNow*, June 17, 2020, https://now.tufts.edu/articles/how-racial-segregation-and-policing-intersect-america.

2   Katelyn Burns, "Why Police Often Single Out Trans People for Violence," Vox, June 23, 2020, https://www.vox.com/identities/2020/6/23/21295432/police-black-trans-people-violence.

DECIDE

It's time.

At some point, you've got to believe that you know enough to give someone a try. Establish the point at which you have done enough discernment. Now it's time to make the call.

BREATHE DEEP . . .

PART III

HOW RACE + GENDER SHOW UP

DURING FINAL HIRING NEGOTIATIONS

You've successfully decided *who* you want to add to your team. Congratulations! In the final part of *Hiring Revolution*, we will dig into the often-overlooked set of tasks that must be successfully accomplished in order to get from making the offer to a staff member's first actual day on the job.

Do you remember how that in-between period felt to you as a worker—you've said "yes" but haven't started yet? It's so stressful! You are busy arranging your departure from your other job—including telling everyone you're leaving, wrapping up final projects, documenting your work, and cleaning up your inbox and contacts lists. Maybe you're figuring out COBRA or managing the intricate timing of prescription refills and doctor's appointments. If you're relocating, the stress increases exponentially. Keep those memories in mind.

Additionally, a work transition means navigating the layers of professional and personal relationships it affects. You might go through a grieving process as you say goodbye to the work you were doing and people you were doing it with. And that's just the stuff you're dealing with during the day! At night you may find yourself on the phone, describing to your family and friends why you felt compelled to make this change, which may or may not feel risky to them.

> *Trina:* If you're anything like me, during this time period your sleep is also getting weird. I lie awake, going over the lengthy to-do list involved in both leaving and beginning anew. When I'm on the precipice of a big work change, my dreams get really vivid—my body, heart, and head conspire while I'm sleeping in an understandable attempt to metabolize what this feels like and to imagine all that may emerge.
>
> It's an intense time, to say the least.

Rather than approaching closing the deal as a mere formality in the hiring process, part III makes space to thoughtfully review the myriad ways that race, religion, class, age, ethnicity, disability, and more create predictive vulnerabilities that should not be glossed over. For example:

- DO NOT underpay people simply because you can get away with it, given their history of being undercompensated for their work and contributions up until this point.
- DO NOT assume you know what benefits are most important to the candidates in your finalist pool.

Building upon what we have already learned about racism and sexism at work, here we will illustrate how cultural preferences for whiteness and masculinity have been threaded into the negotiation and onboarding practices that are considered typical.

As you work to close a deal that is mutually beneficial to you both—the new hire and your company—stay focused on your goals:

1) Hire *this* person.
2) Learn more about *what they need* to be set up for success.
3) Build trust and increase mutual understanding.

In order to get to a yes, remember that this person may or may not need or want what you needed or wanted when you started in a role or company.

Remember—equity is more useful than equality. The exact same onboarding process is not as important as making sure each new employee has what they need (regardless of whether you needed or wanted what you did when you began).

As you work to define and refine starting pay, benefits package, onboarding schedule, and more, get ready to flex your creative and curiosity muscles. Do your best to remain open to what will move you from "this is our selected candidate" to "this person now works here."

CHAPTER 10

THE DAMN DEAL

What follows is a new path you can chart—one rooted in equitable principles and inclusive practices.

At this point, you want to make the call. You want your top candidate to say yes right away, ideally followed by "I can start whenever you need me!" Get in touch with those feelings. In our experiences of hiring, **we often feel some flavor of desperation by the time we get to making the offer—and that can cloud our ability to slow down, get curious, and make sure we are setting up this working relationship for success.**

Notice when and how desperation creeps in. Do you recognize any of the following in yourself?

- "I was ready for someone to start this role yesterday—we're drowning!"
- "I'm desperate to get back to work—hiring is a side hustle to my already full day job!"
- "I really, really, really want them to say yes—they are the person I want!"

Recalling the dominant white cultural pattern of urgency, how do you imagine wanting this process to "just be over with" could cause you to accidentally miss things that are important for your candidate?

You know who you want. Take a breath. Followed by another. And one more still.

You're gonna want this last part to go quickly. But remember: you're committed to equity. You are interested in setting up a long-term relationship with this new employee. Slow down, ask good questions, and stay mindful of all the ways that People of Color, women, and trans people have been relegated to the sidelines and the lowest levels of the US workforce.

Be careful.

We will help you recognize the insidious ways that racism and sexism sneak into final negotiations.

DETAIL + CLARITY

Across lines of difference that make a difference, recognize that common colloquialisms of hiring are not, in fact, imbued with universal shared meaning. For example, "Your pay will be commensurate with experience—that's what feels 'fair' to us." (Real talk: when else does the word *commensurate* ever get used?!) When that's part of your standard language, how might new hires interpret that?

- Does that mean you pay me more the older I am?
- Does that mean you pay someone more than me because they were able to access advanced degrees (that may or may not have direct relevance to the job at hand)?
- Does that mean you are going to base my pay for this role on what other people have paid me in the past?

Do you see how dicey this gets?

Good news: because you've been following the recommendations of *Hiring Revolution* up to the point of making the offer, it is highly likely you have already made your life way easier by sharing relevant details in your job posting and interview process throughout. Here are some additional ways you can proactively reduce barriers to entry for People of Color, women, and trans workers by being specific:

WHAT DO "TRADITIONAL" OFFERS TYPICALLY INCLUDE?

- base rate of pay
- frequency of pay
- days off
- benefits overview (including if union membership is part of this role)
- desired start date
- offer letter making it official

WHAT SHOULD OFFERS INCLUDE, IF YOU ARE SEEKING TO HIRE EQUITABLY?

→ **Staff handbook/personnel policies**—how we do things around here—so new hires can get an even better sense of whether this is somewhere they want to work or not. New hires can infer a lot about how they, personally, will be treated by reading policies. People of Color, women, and trans workers may especially notice dress code, holidays recognized, and work-from-anywhere boundaries, and what those imply about life at your company. For example, allusions to "professional dress" can communicate "We want you to dress and do your hair like a white person" or "We expect you to be gender conforming—and if you're not, it will be a problem."

→ **Detailed information about health benefits**—what we cover and how, including mental health coverage, the cost of specific prescription drugs, paycheck deductions, deductibles, and so on. A lifetime of racism, sexism, and transphobia comes at true costs to our health; if you are planning to hire a mixed-identity team, recognize that you are providing health benefits for people who are more likely to have had little to no access to quality, consistent, affordable health care options over their lifespan. Be clear about what you offer.

→ **Paid Time Off**—explain how time off works and what is considered okay and not okay for frequency and volume of paid days off of work. Practice naming expectations and then practice sticking to them. It is predictable that white and masculine-performing employees might "get away with" informal or unwritten treatment of time off while People of Color, women, and trans people are more likely to get questioned about any activity "off book."

→ **Information about reimbursements and work-related purchases**—what we'll pay for: are mileage/bus fare, parking, phone usage, internet usage, getting a new laptop, and so on covered? People of Color, women, and trans people are more likely to be poor or underpaid, and new costs, such as high-speed home internet or a smartphone, put an actual strain on a familial budget. Although it may feel far outside of your own experience, plan and communicate accordingly.

→ **Expectations about time**—when we work, when we're available by phone/email, and how we arrange time off. Be forthright about exactly what you mean when you talk about your workplace being "flexible" in certain ways. For example, women are still being expected to handle the brunt of community and familial caregiving responsibilities; are people expected to take their own sick days when they have a sick kid or parent?

→ **Protocols for working from outside the office**—when and how we work elsewhere and what's allowed when we do. (CAVEAT: COVID-19 is in the midst of changing both conversations and expectations of businesses and employees when it comes to costs, outputs, and the likely hybrid future of work-from-anywhere possibilities; be prepared to adjust and update this regularly as our collective, and your unique, context shifts and changes.) Try to put aside whether or not *you* prefer working from an office or somewhere else. We lovingly note that this isn't about you. What makes it okay and not okay to work from where? Be specific.

→ **Demographic info about who currently works here**—which you included in the job announcement, and maybe on your website, right? Saying yes to your company includes a curiosity about potentially being the *first* or the *only* in some way—for example, the only Person of Color in the finance department, or the first woman in senior leadership. Every adult gets to decide for themselves whether or not that is something they want to do. Your job is not to omit or fib about reality by going on and on about all the ways your team is diverse. If there are currently no Black people, be honest about that.

→ **How the current org chart works**—and how they, in this role, would fit into it. Remember that inclusion is NOT simply about having a seat at the table—it's about having power enough to change a structure. Titles and org charts can be confusing. Who makes which decisions? Does the chart reflect current reality? And if this person says yes, what would be in their purview and what would not? Be transparent.

Go to www.HiringRevolutionBook.com/Tools to download our **"Equitable Offer" checklist** to make sure you're ready!

During the offering or onboarding phase, watch for a pattern of the new hire asking for a lot more detail than you're providing. Can you be proactive and more open to reviewing the finer points that clearly really matter to this candidate?

WHEN MAKING THE OFFER, CONSIDER THE WHOLE HOUSE

When deciding whether or not to say yes to a job offer, in addition to the tasks of the role, a candidate is also considering how the company will acknowledge, respect, and even value who they are.

In the offer and negotiations part of a hiring process, each of the predictable identity disparities will pop up for you and your candidate in material, relational, and symbolic ways. Consider your whole house and how each identity experience may contribute to a candidate believing this job will or will not be a good fit for them, their families, and their professional development aspirations.

Race

- What is our dress code—our expectations, formalized or not, about how People of Color and white people dress and do their hair, what they smell like, what is considered formal/put together and not, whether hats are allowed in the office or not?
- Who decides what art, what music, what food gets shared in the office?
- What is our company's stance on reacting when an incident of racism happens in our office, building, city, or sector?
- What are our expectations about pronouncing team members' names correctly, and is there accountability for it?
- How will new hires know if they're being paid on par with white people, men, and white men who work here?

Immigration

- Might this person need our workplace to provide sponsorship/visa support?
- If we do direct deposit for paychecks, will pay be accessible for someone operating in cash and not through a traditional bank?
- What is our company's stance on reacting when an incident of xenophobia happens in our office, building, city, or sector?

Trina: I have learned a lot about how different people navigate money differently over the course of my life and career. Consequently, I am mindful of this vast variety of perspectives whenever I am working with a top candidate to get them the compensation package they need to come join us.

One POC friend and colleague shared that her mother, an immigrant and entrepreneur, kept all the family's cash in a kitchen drawer because when she first came to this country, banks took horrible advantage of people in her community. Her mom was living debt free and 100 percent in cash.

Another POC friend and colleague shared with me that their extended family supported one another financially by hiding money in each other's houses whenever they went over. It wasn't a game. The reasoning was humility—the desire not to "take credit" or create a dynamic where relatives "owed" each other anything. It was a way to give with no strings attached.

I myself, a white woman, have vacillated between different class experiences over the course of my life. For quite a while my finances were so tight that my landlord cashing the rent check a day late resulted in me overdrawing my bank account and getting fined. Consequently, I used money orders to pay my rent so that I was certain the money was already out of my account.

My friends, colleagues, and I are all smart, impactful contributors in our jobs. Our financial lives being different, and shifting over time, is in no way an indication of our intellect, value, or worth.

Class

- Do we offer a relocation expense reimbursement package?
- Do we expect new hires to cover expenses of starting employment, such as a uniform or "professional" wardrobe, a laptop, high-speed home internet, and so on?
- Is our office easy to get to on public transportation, or do we expect new hires to have a vehicle, insurance, and funds for gas, repair, maintenance, and parking?

- Do we assume new hires have a passport valid for international travel?
- Do we expect new hires to have a personal credit card with which to cover "incidentals" during business travel?

Language
- What are company preferences around talking with colleagues in languages other than English?
- Who can help translate to ensure understanding of the legal and financial commitments in the offer and acceptance?

Ability
- What does the company, or immediate team lead, need to know about a new person's cognitive, physical, and/or behavioral disabilities or differences if we are to work together?
- Does the company make available particular technology or tools to make work more widely accessible?
- Do you make it a practice to tell all new employees about elevator, ramp, restroom, and stair options in your building?

Age
- What norms has the company established around breast/chest feeding[1] or pumping in the office? During meetings (in person and/or virtual)?
- What is our dress code?
- What expectations do we hold for hours worked? If a weekday schedule is "normal," is working late or over weekends expected or discouraged, and how likely is it? If working unusual or irregular hours is allowed, is it viewed neutrally or assigned judgment?
- Do we treat the presence of a variety of ages as an asset? How do we value employees of different generations?

Religion/Faith
- What dates or holidays do we recognize, celebrate, talk about, or decorate for?

---

1   *Chest feeding* is a term used by some trans men who have mammary glands and are able to feed their babies, but do not consider themselves as having breasts.

- What level of personal religious display (such as specific head coverings, facial hair, clothing items, and hairstyles) is expected or frowned upon?
- How do we navigate faith-related dietary and/or behavior traditions (such as eating Kosher, not consuming alcohol, not touching people of a different gender) in daily exchanges and at company gatherings?

Sexuality

- What is our company's stance on reacting when an incident of homophobia or biphobia[2] happens in our office, building, city, or sector?
- How would you answer the inquiry: "I've been sexually harassed before; how do y'all handle that here, because I want to feel safe?"

Gender

- What are company expectations for working after dark? Working alone in the office? What are our safety and security protocols?
- What are office restrooms and accommodations like (for example, single stall, signed for men/women)?
- How will new hires know if they're being paid on par with men who work here?
- How many people, and what proportion of people in leadership positions, are similar or different to the new hire's current gender presentation?
- What is our practice for sharing and being accountable for using colleagues' pronouns and preferred names?

Ethnicity

- What variances do we have in the way people dress, eat, talk, work, and deal with conflict here?
- What are our expectations about pronouncing team members' names correctly, and is there accountability for it?
- What religious, national, or ethnic traditions does your company acknowledge, honor, or otherwise pay attention to? What about the building your office space is in? (For example, is there a Christmas tree each December in the foyer of the coworking space where you rent a few desks?)

---

2   Transphobia is not included here because being trans is a gender identity, not a sexual orientation.

POWER DYNAMICS ARE SERIOUS—TALK *WITH* INSTEAD OF *AT* PEOPLE DURING NEGOTIATIONS

Once you've made the call and shared the offer, the period of waiting for your top candidate to make their decision can feel particularly unnerving. That's because up until this point in the hiring process, the organization and its hiring professionals have had the bulk of the power. You can say no. Now that power is with the candidate.

Rather than having a take-it-or-leave-it mentality when negotiating the details of the starting package for a new job, can you create the opportunity to be in dialogue? **Trying to "get a good deal" on compensation means missing top talent. Do not underpay people and then expect their passion for your mission to outweigh their financial needs. Pay people well.**

The factors that allow your top candidate to say yes are often *very personal in nature*. The compound impacts of racism, sexism, transphobia, and more are real. **Confidentiality is key throughout the negotiations and compensation package discussions.** As the person responsible for reviewing benefits and the offer in totality, you may learn things that *no one else at your organization ever needs to know*. For example, you might learn, over the course of crafting a starting package, that a candidate:

- has a child with special needs
- has crushing student loan debt,
- has been struggling with fertility issues,
- and more.

Candidates, understandably, may feel that it is dangerous to begin disclosing details about their physical health and financial constraints before officially accepting the offer. However, such details are important to their chances of succeeding in the job and staying with your company. Communicate—and deliver—confidentiality.

ACTIVITY—FEELING FLEXIBLE?

At this point in the process, stay aware of when you are and aren't feeling flexible, about what, and why. Remember that racism and misogyny have wiggled their way into our innermost thought processes. When you catch yourself feeling some flavor of irritated that the person you want to hire is telling you what they need, **Notice** *what's showing up for you:*

- *"They should be grateful we're offering this starting salary, we've never done that before!"*
- *"Why on earth wouldn't they say yes right away? They must have been lying in the interview process about how excited they were!"*
- *"They were so friendly during interviews, but now they feel like a whole new person to me. This negotiation phase is really bringing out another side of them—and I don't like it."*
- *"They probably shouldn't have gotten themselves in so much debt in the first place—the starting salary they claim they need to pay their bills is ridiculous! They should change their lifestyle rather than ask for something so unreasonable."*
- *"They should already have paid into a health savings account if they really have this many health-care needs!"*
- *"It's their fault that they had so many kids. We shouldn't have to pay for their big family."*

Now STOP. Take three deep breaths, each one slower and deeper than the last.

Name: *Where do you think all that came from?*

Why are conversations about this part of this candidate's compensation package setting you off?

- *Are you pissed that they are going to be making more money than you?*
- *Are you overwhelmed that they have so many dependents?*
- *Are you finding it hard to comprehend how they don't already have a car, or high-speed internet at home, or a working iPhone or laptop?*

Journal for five minutes. Write, write, write. Get it all out. Show this writing to no one. You are even welcome to throw it away or shred it the second you're done, if that feels cathartic. This exercise is just for you.

*Once you've observed your own reactions, you can **Navigate** through them to the outcome you really want.*

Whenever you find yourself feeling irritated, annoyed, incredulous, freewrite in order to Notice, Name, and Navigate what is impeding your ability to meet this whole person, your team's top candidate, with nonjudgment, empathy, and kindness.

EQUITABLY MEETING THE NEEDS OF YOUR NEW EMPLOYEE

Your top candidate might be inquiring about something *no other employee has asked you*. That's okay. Try not to assume that their request is impossible to satisfy, or that it's a no or a nonstarter. Do some research and ask industry peers for their help and ideas; consider your boundaries and creative constraints; get honest about where there might be some wiggle room; and see what you can do to figure something out.

Also, remember way back to the myth of fairness. The goal here is not to give everyone exactly what you had, or what the last person who was hired got. Think equity, not equality. For example, at Team Dynamics, when we made different hires, we learned that some staff were already in possession of a functional laptop, while others were not.

The goal is making sure everyone's got what they need to be successful. Don't make folks feel "high maintenance" or "difficult" because they asked for something their colleagues didn't.

NEGOTIATIONS—IDENTITY *ALWAYS* MATTERS

If you are the person responsible for finalizing the top candidate's starting package, it's likely that you feel a lot of responsibility for "getting this deal done" and for "saving our organization some money" where you can. Uff da. If real diversity across lines of meaningful difference is your company's goal, you'll need to reimagine your approach.

If you've followed our revolutionary approach from the beginning of your search, you have already posted your salary or salary range publicly. Your candidate has been aware of it the whole time, which probably made it easier for them to apply because they knew that amount would work for them and their family. Now being upfront about those often hidden details will pay off—big time! We promise this will feel so much better than sharing salary numbers that feel like a surprise far too late in the process. If you haven't been able to do so yet, you can still move toward equity by examining your expectations for the process in advance.

Negotiation, for example, can bring different cultural traditions to the surface. Stop and think: What kinds of judgments do you leap to about different kinds of bodies in negotiation?

What about negotiation when it comes to salary, time off, benefits, or flexible schedule?

Do you come from a cultural tradition or place where negotiating is commonplace? Like haggling in a market to get the best price, or never assuming that the written price will be the final price? Do you come from a cultural tradition where it is considered rude or crass to negotiate or haggle? How do you imagine your comfort and practice (or discomfort and minimal practice) with haggling influences how you approach and experience determining things like starting salary for a job?

Stop and think about what kind of person, in your experience, is allowed or expected to ask for more, and what kind of person is expected to quietly accept what's offered. Consider race. Consider gender. Consider all the combinations of rooms in the Embodied Identity House. Grab paper or open up your digital notes, and consider the following prompts.

ACTIVITY–NEGOTIATIONS
Journal Prompts

How would you feel about a twenty-seven-year-old asking for the top end of the salary range you presented? What reactions can you track yourself having?

How would you feel about a Southeast Asian man telling you he needs the start date to be ninety days from now? What reactions can you track yourself having?

How would you feel about a transgender job candidate asking for a $500 health supplement each month on top of the benefits that go through your insurance carrier? What reactions can you track yourself having?

How would you feel about a woman asking for six paid months off for parental leave in order to say yes to this role? What reactions can you track yourself having?

Once you've Noticed, Named, and Navigated your response to a candidate's request to negotiate, you can respond from the company's needs rather than your own experience and expectations. **Keep in mind that the closer any of us is to living paycheck to paycheck—which People of Color, women, and trans folks are more likely to be—the more every little detail in a compensation package at a new job causes stress and genuinely makes a difference in daily life.** Give them the information they need.

Whether or not the candidate chooses to negotiate, plan to compensate people for the role you are asking them to perform. Whether you are offering the top, middle, or bottom of the range you shared, resist the pressure to get a "deal" because your candidate may have been underpaid in previous jobs. Ten thousand dollars per year, while it might be a tiny fraction of your organization's overall budget, could make a huge difference in the life and health of your candidate and their family. Do not attempt to trim your budget on the backs of People of Color, women, and trans workers. You know what this whole, skilled adult can do for your company: pay accordingly.

ARE YOUR BENEFITS SUPER *WHITE?*

We're really asking. Lifetimes of racism and sexism have predictable consequences for our physical, mental, and emotional health and well-being. When people are healthy and not concerned that one ambulance ride would mean they can't pay their rent, we have better, more focused workers.

Do your benefits policy and coverage packages work for white people better than People of Color? Straight people better than LGBTQ+ people? Cisgender people better than trans people? Middle-class families better than working-class families?

As you delve into the detailed compensation package for your top candidate, based on what they inquire about, **you may become aware, in new ways, that your benefits package was made primarily by white people, for white people, with white people in mind.** What are you, as a workplace, doing to acknowledge and navigate those truths?

Consider
Do you only cover Western/white medicine and healing?

For millennia, different kinds of healing and healers have supported the physical, mental, and psychological health of adults who need to work to live. If your health plan only covers support that is valued by white people, that signals to your workers of color that the way they choose to take care of themselves is seen as "less than" or even "fringe."

Do your current benefits cover:
- chiropractic care
- massage
- reflexology
- reiki
- acupuncture
- acupressure
- cupping
- craniosacral therapy
- and more?

Careful! *Don't blame your insurance provider* on this one! You can choose to provide supplements, advocate with your brokers, and so on to get the benefits your employees use.

Does your company recognize that the US health-care system—no matter how good your benefits are—is rarely inclusive of trans and gender-nonbinary folks' needs?

As more people learn about transgender workers' experiences, some HR professionals are starting to understand where many of the current insurance inadequacies remain. For example, for transgender people who take hormones (which not all people want to do or medically can do safely), results can differ greatly from person to person. If your plan requires that a transgender worker take a generic version of hormones when in fact their body only reacts to the name brand, that worker is not getting their needs met. (You may have had similar experience with birth control, ADHD, anxiety, or depression meds.)

What are you doing to make sure that transgender employees get the support they need to be healthy and well?

Can candidates navigate crushing student loan debt while trying to be a good worker for this company?

There are currently multiple generations in the workforce at the exact same time. Each has had a unique experience with financial aid and access to training and education. As we discussed earlier, many of our younger workers have a monthly student loan payment that is so high it is second only to mortgage or rent in their household budget. Given this unique, daunting, and very common kind of debt (which many people took on specifically to be able to break into the workforce), how can you imagine supporting your workers dealing with this reality, which for many feels impossible to get out from under?

Remember, since People of Color, women, and trans folks are likely to be paid less and have lower lifetime earnings, the impact of student loan debt exacerbates precarious financial positions for those workers especially.

Immigration Status

As a company, you are legally allowed to employ anyone who is federally "eligible" to work. Individual and family immigration and forced migration circumstances are often complex (for example, for refugees, asylum seekers, and binational couples). A worker not born in the United States may be eligible to work because they have a visa, are naturalized, have become a citizen, and/ or are covered by a provision such as Deferred Action for Childhood Arrivals (DACA).

Did you know that US employers are among the fiercest advocates for comprehensive immigration reform because they find it profoundly irritating to be prevented from hiring and retaining top talent? There are a limited number of particular visa renewals, even for "highly skilled workers" such as doctors and engineers.

If you have not sponsored a worker for a visa before, there are resources to help you navigate that process. Check with US Citizenship and Immigration Services, your state employment department, or advocacy organizations such as Immigration Equality for more information.

As you get closer to that yes, make note of when and how your candidate made you think differently. Which questions did they have for you that required you to look up or research the answer? Which of your current company policies inspired the most questions or requests for clarification? Choose to learn from each negotiation and onboarding planning process. Plan to revisit these opportunities for increased creativity, knowledge, and specificity on your part. If you revisit and revise, when the time comes to hire your next new employee, you'll be ready to position your organization as an even more welcoming and equitable workplace.

LETTING PEOPLE DOWN WHILE STILL BUILDING RELATIONSHIPS

In order to say yes to your top candidate, you have to say no to all others. Recognizing the hard work you put into reaching new and different communities, and the new relationships you built along the way, it would be a total shame to just let those relationships fade. Your finalist pool was made up of highly qualified folks, and chances are, you can envision them fitting somewhere in your organization soon or in the future.

Be thoughtful about expanding your network of incredible professionals, even at this stage. **Once you get a yes and your new hire has signed on the dotted line, circle back to the folks in your finalist pool to share the news and to stay connected.** At Team Dynamics, we do that by phone or by email. Here is an example of a recent email Alfonso sent letting folks know we didn't select them:

> *Hello!*
> *Thanks for your patience while we deliberated about our VP role. I'll start up top by saying we did not move you forward after our last interview. We are so grateful for the work and energy you put into the process.*
> *We were so humbled to have you in the mix. We are making sure to connect with folks who are in our network and community already and important to us. It was tough not to move you forward, especially knowing how excited folks get to apply for something.*
> *We had an overwhelming response and we are blown away by all the folks who want to work with us in this time of growth. We think really highly of you as a leader and as a manager and hope our work continues to intersect.*
> *Thank you,*
> *Alfonso*

And here is an example of one of the real-life responses we received:

> Hi Alfonso & Trina,
> Thank you very much for your email. While admittedly it was not what I was hoping for, I am very grateful for the opportunity to interview with you and for the transparency in your process. I wish you amazing growth and success, and look forward to bumping into each other in the future.

The lesson here is to be thoughtful and proactive. Stay connected to the professional pool, especially the People of Color, women, and trans people you met along your way. **It is possible to stay in good relationship with folks you choose not to hire** when you do the work to honor their time, contributions, and vulnerability for trying out with you at all.

CHAPTER 11

WHY YOU NEED TO ASK
RATHER THAN ASSUME
WHAT NEW HIRES NEED

Imagine, after weeks (maybe even months) of dreaming about who would eventually become your newest colleague, it's time for your new staff member's first day. In our world, the new staffer's first day marks the completion of the hiring process. Congratulations!

From their first day forward, **your focus becomes building a working relationship that works**. This person is no longer "trying out" for the role, so make certain they are not being treated that way. Some old-school cultural dynamics often linger around new folks needing to "prove themselves": let go of that old way of thinking and behaving.

Diversifying your team across lines of race, gender, and more requires that you stay alert to dynamics of your staff as their working relationships develop, grow, and deepen. Remember, your goal isn't for different kinds of people to join your team, only for them all to be expected to *act the same!*

CONSIDER YOUR WELCOME

Think about the first days you've had over the course of your life: first days of school, first days on a new team, first dates. What do firsts have in common?

> *Trina:* For me, "firsts" bring up an intense mix of emotions: excitement, anticipation, fear, curiosity, and more. In a nutshell, I am anxious to finally get started, and I am hoping to God that I don't embarrass myself or mess things up.

Remember back to your first day working at the company you're at now:

- How long ago was that?
- What do you remember from that day?
- What was your day like before you logged in/went into the office?
- How was your first day spent?
- Who did you meet and start to get to know?
- What memory from that first day sticks with you still today?
- How did you feel when you went home/logged off after that first day?

DON'T GUESS—INSTEAD, ASK + OFFER

On a new staff member's first day, it can feel very easy to simply ***project what you would want*** your first day to be like onto your newest colleague. Be careful! Find out what *they* want it to be like.

- Do they want a big fuss to be made? Or would they prefer to slip into the background?
- Do they want to do "get to know you" activities with other staff, or does that feel too vulnerable given that they still haven't met everyone?

What feels welcoming, hospitable, and inclusive is unique from person to person.

Now imagine welcoming a Person of Color, woman, and/or trans staff member who is the first or only on their work team, in your office, or at that particular level of leadership. What can and should you do to make them feel truly welcome? **Ask. Offer. Don't assume.**

Keeping in mind the relevance of identity to our onboarding experience, consider the concerns *they* might be having. For example:

- If folks aren't used to pronouncing a name like mine, can we build **pronunciation tips** into my email signature when we set up my account? Would other people be willing to add pronunciation tips as well, or will I be the only one?
- Does **physical touch** (handshakes, hugs, cheek kisses) work for me or not, or just sometimes, in a work setting? How do I like to be greeted, and what is out of bounds for me?
- Are there **single-stall restrooms**? Do they require special keys or key cards? Who has access to those, and who is expected to use bathrooms separated by a gender binary?

USE YOUR *EMBODIED IDENTITY HOUSE* TOOL TO PRACTICE STOPPING IN EACH ROOM:

Based on what you may know about the religious tradition of your new colleague, have you accidentally asked them to start on a holy or sacred day? **Ask. Offer. Don't assume.**

Based on their immigration experience, do you have all the paperwork ready for renewing their H-1B visa as a highly skilled worker, sponsored by your company? **Ask. Offer. Don't assume.**

Based on their disabilities/abilities, have you purchased the correct monitor for their workstation so they are able to see script and contrast clearly? **Ask. Offer. Don't assume.**

You don't need to know *everything* about a person's lived experience and full set of needs the moment they join you. What you can do is proactively offer accommodations and resources to set them up for success as best as possible.

PREPARING YOUR STAFF TO RECEIVE AND SUPPORT YOUR PICK

As you diversify your staff across lines of race, gender, and more, consider how you're bringing everyone along in growing and changing with the addition of this new person. If we aren't intentional about stopping, discussing, and dreaming together about how to create a more equitable and inclusive first few days, weeks, and months as a company, we risk doing all this work in hiring, only to reinforce workplace practices that preference whiteness and masculinity, thus sending a message to a new hire that *how* they are is not, in fact, welcome. How can you help your team and new colleague get off to a good start together? Be proactive.

Staff retention is a whole other book, but for now, here are some things you can do to make sure the welcome you offer doesn't just repeat the way you experienced it (whether that worked for you or not).

Notice and name the expectations you have for the rest of your staff's behavior with this new person. Remember, there is value in being explicit, especially if your expectations of staff supporting a new person's onboarding are changing and evolving over time.

For example:

- I expect you to send a friendly welcome email their first day as a reply-all to my announcement email.
- I expect you to stop by their desk and introduce yourself on their first day and offer to be available for questions about how the office works.
- I expect you to invite the person to eat lunch with you.

Be clear, rather than facing disappointment when folks don't rise to the occasion you've set in your head. Even if the definition of "welcoming behavior" on someone's first day feels like common sense to you, chances are the majority of your workers are focused on their own tasks. If they are not paying attention, it's likely not because they don't care about this new staff person; rather, it's just one item in a set of data they are navigating in their busy day.

Also, a predominantly white and masculine-presenting team may not be aware of the additional stress People of Color, women, and trans people are holding on the first day as the first, one of a few, or part of a growing group of People of Color, women, and trans workers.

FIRST-DAY DOS AND DON'TS WITH YOUR NEWEST HIRE

Do	Don't
Ask what would work well for them on day one	Assume you know what would work best
Review what a day in the office is like	Assume that your norm is the universal common-sense, preferred, or only good way to approach a role
Clarify boundaries: what is and isn't okay in email, on Slack, in meetings, in a workday, with clients/customers, etc.	Wait for people to do something you find off-putting to share work boundaries
Prioritize relationship building at least as much as task training	Fixate on task teaching at the expense of building relationships and relationship capital
Make sure they get to meet different folks	Stick them with one person they must gel with, or else
Stay curious and remain open to learning more about what they need to be set up for success	Assume that just because we haven't responded to a request before, we cannot do it
Remember the value of quality in relationships, not just the quantity of coworkers' names a new staff member can memorize their first week.	Fixate on speed of the first few days and weeks when you are wanting a years-long relationship with this person—keep the beginning in that broader and truer context
What else do you think of?	

Lastly, be mindful that US-based workplaces, because of an undercurrent of sexism, often assign women and feminine-presenting people to "take good care" of new employees. Don't assume that only these folks are primed to do the emotional labor of onboarding. Expect men to be proactive, curious, and caring as well.

Notice assumptions you've made about who is the most friendly and who a new staff member will like the best or think is the most fun to be around. This set of assumptions can be raced, gendered, and classed, and it includes assumptions about "personality style" that are also related to cultural practices and preferences. For example, recognize that quiet people are not worse at being friendly, they're just quiet.

When connecting new folks to guides or mentors—we've shared this before!—**Ask. Offer. Don't assume.** Don't assign a new employee a Black "buddy" just because your new staffer is Black. Same holds true for assigning women to women, or LGBTQ+ people to LGBTQ+ people. In determining what sort of peer connection or mentorship your new colleague might need or want, begin with curiosity. *Have you spoken with them about the identity mix of the team and the company? Do you know if they'd like to be introduced proactively to peers or mentors of like or different identities? What are your motivations or assumptions related to finding a "buddy" for someone?* If you have a more formal mentorship or affinity support group for staff of different identities, keep that explicit. Think about the mix of who you want your new staff member to get to know early and why. Do not pigeonhole new staff into only a certain set of working relationships.

FROM THE FIRST DAY THROUGH THE FIRST FEW WEEKS

Inclusion is self-reported—meaning, I don't get to proclaim, "I was so inclusive!" Why? Because this doesn't take into account how the person you were intending to include actually feels. Each person we hire, onboard, and work with can let us know if and when they feel set up for success, listened to, valued, and more.

First impressions matter. Solid working relationships and trust are built over time. Most likely, you will learn more about your new colleague, and they about you, in a mix of planned and organic ways.

Be mindful that some of your colleagues who are People of Color, women, and trans folks will be feeling the extra pressure to "represent" entire groups of workers like them. One of the often overlooked benefits of whiteness is that individuals are judged as individuals. **For many People of Color, women, and trans people in the workforce, especially in leadership, it can feel as though everyone is watching to see how they do, if they fit in, and what they're like to be around**—and what happens is, inside of racist and sexist systems, group bias toward or away from people in these groups gets reinforced.

One of the added benefits of joining the Hiring Revolution is having dialogue early and often with your newest colleague about how identity is always present and relevant at work. Build on that practice in the first few weeks of a new colleague's tenure rather than dancing around truths like being the first or only. **Be brave enough to regularly ask open-ended questions about how work is going and what you and your team could be doing to make it even better.**

Resist asking questions that are likely to get you surface-level answers and instead ask constructive, thoughtful questions. For example:

> *Generic question: Did you have fun today? (It sounds like they're expected to answer yes.)*
>
> *Specific alternatives: What stood out to you from that mid-day meeting? What are you feeling most curious about after today? What are you wanting to dig into next?*
>
> *Generic question: Isn't he great? (A leading question)*
>
> *Specific alternatives: James told you today about the projects you'll collaborate on. What ideas or curiosity came up for you about those projects or how you're expect to partner with James?*

From entering the office or logging in, to leaving or logging off at the end of the work week, one of the best practices you can develop early on is regularly asking specific questions and really listening to how your work culture is working for your newest staff members.

THE RESPONSIBILITY OF REVOLUTIONARIES

You've made it this far in this book. That tells us you're a revolutionary. *We're so excited!*

Maybe you've never thought of yourself as a revolutionary before. Maybe you've always thought of yourself that way!

Either way, **your commitment to righting the wrongs that have been done because of racism and sexism embedded in hiring practices tells us that you have a lot of clarity about making workplaces better.**

At this point you might be feeling a mix of freaked out, motivated, excited, and overwhelmed. We made *Hiring Revolution* a guide in order to quell the overwhelm. We know many of you, especially in HR/talent development, are being asked to "diversify the talent pool," "diversify your staff," and/or "take an equitable and/or anti-racist approach to hiring." Deep breath. Those are BIG, overarching goals that require the wholesale pulling apart of the old way and putting back together the new way.

To get re-grounded before you head out to make change, we thought we should close out with an important question: *What is the responsibility of revolutionaries?*

START NOW—DON'T WAIT FOR SOMEONE ELSE TO TAKE THE LEAD

You may or may not be the only person at your current organization who knows how abysmally biased traditional hiring processes are. Whatever your colleagues' current state of awareness, do NOT *wait* for someone else to give you "permission" to start hiring equitably.

If, like us, you are hiring on a regular basis, the sooner you can put some, any, or all of the *Hiring Revolution* recommendations into your practice, the quicker you'll be able to catch preferences for whiteness and masculinity and better live your values. One task at a time, one moment to the next, practice what this book teaches you: Investigate Your Instincts; Notice, Name, and Navigate; and rebuild applications, hiring committees, interview questions, and how you make final decisions, one component at a time.

Each change you make may feel small alone. But together, these changes will ultimately steer your big ship on a much better course!

Revolutions are goal directed: Keep your eyes on the prize! The goal is to have a hiring process you can feel proud of.

Revolutions are *not* free-for-alls. Revolutions are specific. Even if you're not at liberty to rewrite your whole hiring process at once, the following three questions will help you build a practice that adds up to meaningful change. Ask yourself:

- **What are we going to STOP doing?** Because it does harm, it leaves people out, it hurts folks, it has a negative impact on our committee and/or candidates, and/or it doesn't get us measurably closer to our goals.
- **What are we going to START doing?** Even on a trial basis! What are we willing to try, and why? If we started _____, how would that improve our process, interactions, ability to make a decision between qualified adults, etc.? Put another way, if we skip or don't do _____, what do we risk missing?
- **What are we going to do BETTER/DIFFERENTLY?** If we tweaked this part of the job description, this application question, this part of the interview, this aspect of the rubric, what would be improved? How can our thinking and behavior evolve to better meet the needs of our candidates and committees?

Remember: revolutions are bound to include both *breakdowns* and *breakthroughs*.

As you lead, drive, and contribute to your workplace's Hiring Revolution, there will be plenty of moments worth celebrating. There will also be setbacks—large and small. When you experience frustration (maybe because you can't get your org to proactively post salaries, or you're struggling to get a hiring committee to stop talking about biased notions of "favorite" and "likability"), take heart in the fact that revolutions involve falling down and getting back up again. Dr. Brené Brown talks in her books about the capacity to "Rise Strong"—recognizing tenacity and stick-to-it-iveness as a core leadership capacity needed in modern workplaces.

Revolutions are not singular acts or declarations. Revolutions are a *series of sustained and strategic actions.*

Moment to moment, conversation to conversation, decision to decision, your Hiring Revolution will be successful as you continue to *practice* increasingly equitable approaches to your process. **When you are feeling stuck about what to do or try next, revisit your goals and your process piece by piece, identifying the next good and right and values-aligned thing you can try *today.***

Stay creative. Be solution focused. And ask for help. If one part of your Hiring Revolution feels like it is stalling, *regroup, reimagine, and reengage.* What *can* you try next? If giving up isn't an option (which it isn't, because racism and sexism in hiring are GROSS and have DEVASTATING results), what can you try today, tomorrow, next week, and with the help of the team of revolutionaries you continue to recruit and rely on? You don't have to do it alone!

FINAL REMINDER: ROLE, GOAL, AND SOUL

We introduced this framework in chapter 4. It helps us stay true to course—especially when it's hard, especially when it's cumbersome and complex, especially when we need courage to change a pattern, to move away from the way we've always done things, and take a leap. Time and time again, we anchor to our values, our purpose, and our unique opportunity by revisiting:

- What is our **role?**
- What is our **goal?**
- How do we get there without losing our **soul?**

Ask yourself these questions regularly and you will keep making progress.

To anyone who has wondered, What on earth can I do about centuries of racism and sexism?, the answer is, This! You can do this. You can be part of the United States Hiring Revolution. This entire book is an offering. It is an invitation that we hope you choose to accept. This book charts a course for a future we can be very proud of.

Hiring Revolutionaries commit, time and time again, to the daily, weekly, and yearly actions required to bend that arc toward justice. Your arms will get tired, and the arc will try to bounce back into its original shape. Build a team, pull like hell, and be unrelenting in your pursuit. Together, we can be the working generation that revolutionizes how we find, recruit, and hire our dream teams!

In Solidarity, with Much Love + Respect,

WORK LIFE *AFTER* YOU HIRE—GETTING YOUR DREAM TEAM IN THE DOOR AND RETAINING THEM OVER TIME

Our goal for *Hiring Revolution* is to help you build and execute a hiring process you feel genuinely proud of. You are welcome to reach out to us at any time to learn more about how we can work side by side with you and your team to take what you've learned from *Hiring Revolution* and expand that knowledge to apply everything you've learned: team@teamdynamicsmn.com and www.TeamDynamicsMN.com are the best ways to reach us.

Because equity in hiring is one facet of our holistic suite of services, a lot of folks have already asked us, "So, once I hire someone awesome, how can I make sure that they stay?" That's the right question. Given the ever-present realities of racism and sexism, the next areas of focus are, rightfully, *staff retention* and *team culture*.

We're happy to help. Reach out. We're called to do this work and happy to do it alongside you.

GRATITUDE

Gratitude to our publishing partners at Wise Ink, especially Dara Beevas, for insisting this book was needed. Special thanks to Kellie Hultgren for diligently editing this text—making our thoughts and words increasingly clear. Thank you for caring about us, caring about this, and sharing your wisdom so we could share ours.

Gratitude to our Team Dynamics crew! Thank you for saying yes when we hired each of you. Incredible colleagues can change your life—our colleagues have certainly changed ours.

Gratitude to our peers, mentors, elders, and ancestors. We are alive, alert, and awake during this movement moment, taking the baton during this leg of the race. We listened, we learned, we work to make you proud, and we continue to carry what you've taught us forward. Thank you for investing in us.

To our teams over the course of our careers, especially our LGBTQ+ movement fam, thank you.

From Alfonso: Thanks to Jan, Jaz, Dana, and LP, my rocks, for the whole adventure, this one and all the others. Twin Cousin, for being a constant. Mom/Dad/Am/Tone, for saying yes and showing up. Deb, for inviting me to grow up. Beth and Nehrwr, for teaching me the IDC way. Anyone who ever interacted with the Ron McKinley Fellows program, for teaching me hard lessons about hiring. Greg Grinley, for showing me my first act of revolutionary hiring when he picked me. Trina, for absolutely believing this book was possible and for driving it.

From Trina: Jack and Abbie, our friendships, including when you push me to be my best self, are why I am able to take big risks with my life and my heart. Mom, Dad, Breen, and Patrick—thank you for showing me in ways large and small that you care about what I feel called to do. To my incomparable nieces: Ruona, Hannah, and Sarai, the three of you inspire me to create a better world. Thank you for the unique way you share your love regardless of how good I am at my job. To my Task Force family, for raising me in a movement committed to race and gender equity. To LP, RK, DN, JM, and Fastner—y'all make me feel sane and never ever alone. To Deb, Jillian, Bryan, Dr. Kayla, Dr. Sherry, Dr. Johnson—thank you for keeping my body, mind, and spirit working the past two years so I could complete this project. Alfonso, for saying out loud that we should just start writing this damn book, for making me laugh, and for teaching and inspiring me each and every day.

We are honored by the opportunity to put this call to action out into the world. Thank YOU!

TOOLS + RESOURCES

MORE FROM THE AUTHORS
Book website: www.HiringRevolutionBook.com
BEHAVE Podcast
www.TeamDynamicsMN.com

RECOMMENDATIONS FOR FURTHER LEARNING
Podcasts
Scene on Radio
The Peabody-nominated podcast from the Center for Documentary Studies (CDS) at Duke University, *www.sceneonradio.org*, especially:
- Season 2: "Seeing White"
- Season 3: "MEN"
- Season 4: "The Land That Never Has Been Yet"

Hosted and produced by John Biewan. Seasons 2 and 4 also include regular contributions by Dr. Chenjerai Kumanyika. Season 3 is cohosted by Celeste Headlee.

Keep It
Hosted by Ira Madison III, Louis Virtel, and Aida Osman: "a show about pop culture, politics, and what happens when they smack into each other at alarming speed." *www.crooked.com/podcast-series/keep-it*

Lovett or Leave It
Hosted by former Obama speechwriter Jon Lovett: "Quizzes! Impressions! Shouting at cable news clips! And everyone's favorite: nuanced discussion." *www.crooked.com/podcast-series/lovett-or-leave-it/*

adrienne maree brown
author, scholar, and activist. Check out her work at *www.adriennemareebrown.net*, especially:
- *Emergent Strategy*
- *Pleasure Activism*
- *We Will Not Cancel Us*
- Instagram @ adriennemareebrown

"White Supremacy Culture,"
an article by Tema Okun, at *www.dismantlingracism.org*. We encourage all of our clients to read this as background for our work.

Unapologetic: A Black, Queer, and Feminist Mandate for Radical Movements,
by Charlene A. Carruthers
The five questions she poses changed our lives. You should read it too! *www.charlenecarruthers.com/unapologetic*

TRINA C. OLSON

Trina Olson is the next guiding voice in the conversation about the future of work and equitable work culture. CEO and cofounder of Team Dynamics, Trina believes going to work in America can feel fundamentally different if—and only if—we deal with the impacts of racism and sexism. After the murder of George Floyd, Trina crafted a curriculum for white leaders, including the staff of Senator Bernie Sanders, to process and plan (without burdening POC colleagues). For the past twenty-five years Trina has held key leadership roles around the country in New York, Seattle, Los Angeles, and Washington, DC. A two-time executive director, she has lobbied the White House, raised millions of dollars, and effectively mobilized for major policy and culture change.

Trina has authored and coauthored numerous pieces on race and gender issues, including "Seeking Safe Haven: LGBTQ People and the American Immigration Experience." She's a cohost on the BEHAVE podcast and a highly sought-after workplace equity advisor.

ALFONSO T. WENKER

Alfonso Wenker is a lauded movement and thought leader driven to convene, connect, and coach top executives to better align values with practice. President and cofounder of Team Dynamics, Alfonso is focused on organizing mixed teams to cocreate new paradigms for how people can work and lead. During the historic campaign for the freedom to marry, Alfonso was recruited and served as the deputy finance director for Minnesotans United for All Families. As a third-generation Mexican American, queer, Catholic man living in Minneapolis, Alfonso consistently gathers and responds to communities calling for racial justice and gender liberation. Before Team Dynamics, Alfonso's career centered in philanthropy, where for over a decade he worked tirelessly to equitably steward billions in resources, while creating new opportunities for People of Color to break into and lead in the field.

Alfonso's considerable body of work has been recognized through being awarded Minneapolis/St. Paul Business Journal's 40 Under 40, MCN's Catalytic Leader, and St. Paul Foundation's Facing Race Anti-Racism Award.

TEAM DYNAMICS

Team Dynamics is a national race and gender justice firm providing training, coaching, and strategy support for workers and workplaces. A People of Color-, woman-, and LGBTQ+-owned business, Team Dynamics is purposefully comprised of interdisciplinary adult educators and intercultural capacity building specialists.

Committed to workplace transformation, Team Dynamics has founded its practice on racial equity-centered leadership development, helping clients build the necessary capacity to navigate race, gender, disability, and more in contemporary workplaces. To date, Team Dynamics has successfully supported more than one hundred companies, ranging from architecture firms to opera houses, colleges to faith communities, athletics to philanthropy.

Currently, Team Dynamics is called on to support clients such as *On Being*'s Krista Tippett, Clockwork's Nancy Lyons, and countless HR executives nationwide. www.TeamDynamicsMN.com